PIANO • VOCAL • GUITAR

THE GRAMMY

BEST COUNTRY SONG
1964 - 2011

®

Visit The Recording Academy Online at
www.grammy.com

ISBN 978-1-4584-1564-6

HAL•LEONARD®
CORPORATION
7777 W. Bluemound Rd. P.O. Box 13819 Milwaukee, WI 53213

Visit Hal Leonard Online at
www.halleonard.com

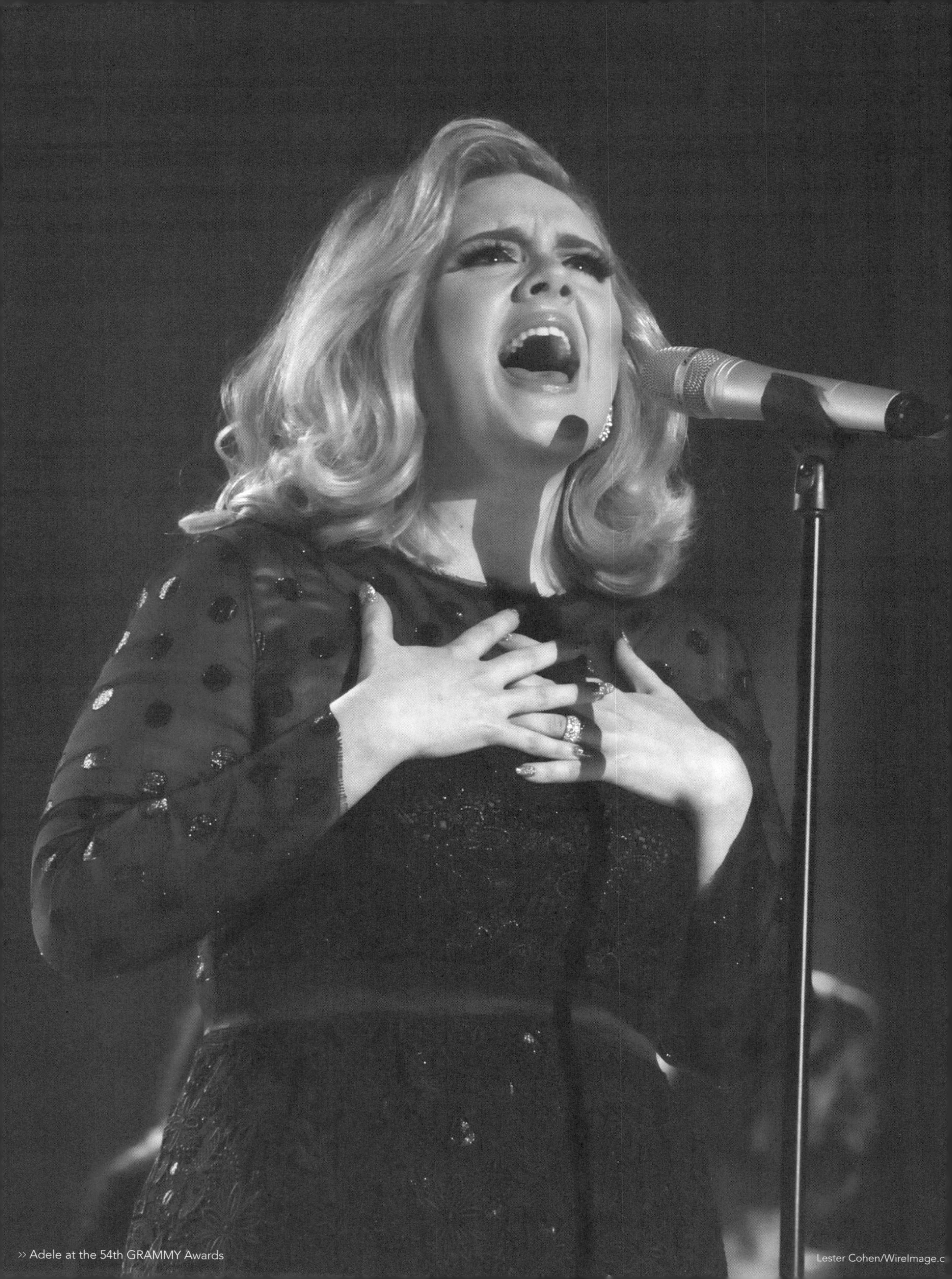

›› Adele at the 54th GRAMMY Awards

Lester Cohen/WireImage.c

THE RECORDING ACADEMY®

When it comes to music on TV, the last few years alone have seen some very memorable moments: Paul McCartney, Bruce Springsteen, Dave Grohl, and Joe Walsh jamming on "The End" from the Beatles' classic *Abbey Road*; Adele making her triumphant first live singing appearance after throat surgery to perform "Rolling In The Deep"; Pink dripping wet and hovering 20 feet above the stage while singing a note-perfect version of "Glitter In The Air"; and Lady Gaga hatching from a massive egg to perform "Born This Way." All of these performances, and many more, took place on the famed GRAMMY Awards® stage.

The GRAMMY® Award is indisputedly the most coveted recognition of excellence in recorded music worldwide. Over more than half a century, the GRAMMY Awards have become both music's biggest honor and Music's Biggest Night®, with the annual telecast drawing tens of millions of viewers nationwide and millions more internationally.

And with evolving categories that always reflect important current artistic waves — such as dance/electronica music — as well as setting a record for social TV engagement in 2012, the GRAMMYs keep moving forward, serving as a real-time barometer of music's cultural impact.

The Recording Academy is the organization that produces the GRAMMY Awards. Consisting of the artists, musicians, songwriters, producers, engineers, and other professionals who make the music you enjoy every day on the radio, your streaming or download services, or in the concert hall, The Academy is a dynamic institution with an active agenda aimed at supporting and nurturing music and the people who make it.

Whether it's joining with recording artists to ensure their creative rights are protected, providing ongoing professional development services to the recording community or supporting the health and well-being of music creators and music education in our schools, The Recording Academy has become the recording industry's primary organization for professional and educational outreach, human services, arts advocacy, and cultural enrichment.

The Academy represents members from all corners of the professional music world — from the biggest recording stars to unsung music educators — all brought together under the banner of building a better creative environment for music and its makers.

>> Paul McCartney at the 2012 MusiCares Person of the Year gala in his honor

Christopher Polk/WireImage.c

>> Trombone Shorty and Mavis Staples at the GRAMMY Foundation's Music Preservation Project event in 2012

Michael Kovac/WireImage.

MUSICARES FOUNDATION®

MusiCares® was established by The Recording Academy to provide a safety net of critical assistance for music people in times of need. MusiCares has developed into a premier support system for music people, providing resources to cover a wide range of financial, medical and personal emergencies through innovative programs and services, including regular eBay auctions of one-of-a-kind memorabilia that are open to the public. The charity has been supported by the contributions and participation of artists such as Neil Diamond, Aretha Franklin, Paul McCartney, Bruce Springsteen, Barbra Streisand, and Neil Young — just to name the organization's most recent annual Person of the Year fundraiser honorees — and so many others through the years.

THE GRAMMY FOUNDATION®

The GRAMMY Foundation's mission is to cultivate the understanding, appreciation and advancement of the contribution of recorded music to American culture. The Foundation accomplishes this mission through programs and activities designed to engage the music industry and cultural community as well as the general public. The Foundation works to bring national attention to important issues such as the value and impact of music and arts education and the urgency of preserving our rich cultural legacy, and it accomplishes this work by engaging music professionals — from big-name stars to working professionals and educators — to work directly with students.

>> Secretary of the Department of Health and Human Services Kathleen Sebelius and Recording Academy President/CEO Neil Portnow present the Recording Artists' Coalition Award to John Mayer at the GRAMMYs on the Hill Awards in Washington, D.C. in 2012

Paul Morigi/WireImage.c

FIGHTING FOR MUSICIANS' RIGHTS

Over the last 15 years, The Recording Academy has built a presence in the nation's capital, working to amplify the voice of music creators in national policy matters. Today, called the "supersized musicians lobby" by *Congressional Quarterly*, The Academy's Advocacy & Industry Relations office in Washington, D.C., is the leading representative of the collective world of recording professionals — artists, songwriters, producers, and engineers — through its GRAMMYs on the Hill® Initiative. The Academy has taken a leadership role in the fight to expand radio performance royalties to all music creators, worked on behalf of musicians on censorship concerns and regularly supported musicians on legislative issues that impact the vitality of music.

THE GRAMMY MUSEUM®

Since opening its doors in December 2008, the GRAMMY Museum has served as a dynamic educational and interactive institution dedicated to the power of music. The four-story, 30,000-square foot facility is part of L.A. Live, the premier sports and entertainment destination in downtown Los Angeles. The Museum serves the community with interactive, permanent and traveling exhibits and an array of public and education programs. We invite you to visit us when you're in the Los Angeles area.

As you can see, The Recording Academy is so much more than the annual GRAMMY telecast once a year, even if that one show is Music's Biggest Night. To keep up with all The Academy's activities, visit GRAMMY.com regularly, and join the conversation on our social networks:

Facebook.com/TheGRAMMYs

Twitter.com/TheGRAMMYs

YouTube.com/TheGRAMMYs

TheGRAMMYs.tumblr.com

Foursquare.com/TheGRAMMYs

Instagram (user name: TheGRAMMYs)

Google+ (gplus.to/TheGRAMMYs)

TABLE OF CONTENTS (ALPHABETICAL)

PAGE	TITLE	ARTIST	YEAR
126	I Still Believe In You	**Vince Gill**	1992
107	I Swear	**John Michael Montgomery**	1994
130	It's Five O'Clock Somewhere	**Alan Jackson & Jimmy Buffett**	2003
136	Jesus, Take The Wheel	**Carrie Underwood**	2006
142	King Of The Road	**Roger Miller**	1965
144	Kiss An Angel Good Mornin'	**Charley Pride**	1972
147	Little Green Apples	**Roger Miller and O.C. Smith**	1968
152	Live Like You Were Dying	**Tim McGraw**	2004
174	Love Can Build A Bridge	**The Judds**	1991
163	Mean	**Taylor Swift**	2011
180	My Woman, My Woman, My Wife	**Marty Robbins**	1970
184	Need You Now	**Lady Antebellum**	2010
190	9 To 5	**Dolly Parton**	1981
194	On The Road Again	**Willie Nelson**	1980
198	Passionate Kisses	**Mary Chapin Carpenter**	1993
210	Stay	**Sugarland**	2008
216	Stranger In My House	**Ronnie Milsap**	1983
222	A Very Special Love Song	**Charlie Rich**	1974
226	Where Were You (When The World Stopped Turning)	**Alan Jackson**	2002
234	Where've You Been	**Kathy Mattea**	1990
203	White Horse	**Taylor Swift**	2009
238	You Decorated My Life	**Kenny Rogers**	1979
242	You're Still The One	**Shania Twain**	1998

TABLE OF CONTENTS (CHRONOLOGICAL)

* Omitted due to licensing restrictions.

YEAR	PAGE	TITLE	ARTIST
1988	112	**Hold Me**	K.T. Oslin
1989	12	**After All This Time**	Rodney Crowell
1990	234	**Where've You Been**	Kathy Mattea
1991	174	**Love Can Build A Bridge**	The Judds
1992	126	**I Still Believe In You**	Vince Gill
1993	198	**Passionate Kisses**	Mary Chapin Carpenter
1994	107	**I Swear**	John Michael Montgomery
1995	89	**Go Rest High On That Mountain**	Vince Gill
1996	40	**Blue**	LeAnn Rimes
1997	48	**Butterfly Kisses**	Bob Carlisle
1998	242	**You're Still The One**	Shania Twain
1999	62	**Come On Over**	Shania Twain
2000	118	**I Hope You Dance**	Lee Ann Womack
2001	*	**The Lucky One**	Alison Krauss & Union Station
2002	226	**Where Were You (When The World Stopped Turning)**	Alan Jackson
2003	130	**It's Five O'Clock Somewhere**	Alan Jackson & Jimmy Buffett
2004	152	**Live Like You Were Dying**	Tim McGraw
2005	30	**Bless The Broken Road**	Rascal Flatts
2006	136	**Jesus, Take The Wheel**	Carrie Underwood
2007	22	**Before He Cheats**	Carrie Underwood
2008	210	**Stay**	Sugarland
2009	203	**White Horse**	Taylor Swift
2010	184	**Need You Now**	Lady Antebellum
2011	163	**Mean**	Taylor Swift

AFTER ALL THIS TIME

Words and Music by
RODNEY CROWELL

E
end - ing.
spo - ken.
There was
There were
time and we were burn - ing,
ways I should have thrilled you.
There were
There were
C♯m7
rhymes and we were learn - ing.
days when I could have killed you.
There was
You're the
A
B
E
all the love two hearts could hold.
on - ly love my life has known.

A
And af - ter all ___ this time, you're
And af - ter all ___ this time, you're
Instrumental solo
G♯m
al - ways on my mind. ___ Hey,
al - ways on my mind. ___ Hey,
Solo ends
And
A
F♯m
I could nev - er let it end, 'cause my heart takes so long to mend. The
I could nev - er let you go, a bro - ken heart that heals so slow, could
I could nev - er let it in, 'cause my heart takes so long to mend. The
B
A/B
B
dream that keeps your hopes ___ a - live, the lone - ly nights ___ you hold in - side. ___ And
nev - er beat for some - one new while you're a - live ___ and I am too. ___ And
dream that keeps your hopes ___ a - live, the lone - ly nights ___ you hold in - side. ___ And

A
B
af - ter all this time, you're al - ways on my mind. I still
af - ter all this time, you're al - ways on my mind. I still
af - ter all this time, you're al - ways on my mind. I still
E
To Coda
1
2
D.S. al Coda
want you. There was
miss you.
want you.
CODA
A
Hey, af - ter all this time, you're
B
N.C.
E
B
A
E
al - ways on my mind. I still love you.

ALMOST PERSUADED

Words and Music by
GLENN SUTTON and BILLY SHERRILL

E♭ 3fr
A♭ 4fr
A♭7 4fr
hand. She had ru - by red lips,
mine. I found my - self want - ing to
man." Then I looked in - to her eyes and I
D♭
A♭ 4fr
E♭7
coal black hair and eyes that would tempt an - y
kiss her for temp - ta - tion was flow - ing like
saw it. The re - flec - tion of my wed - ding
A♭ 4fr
1
E♭ 3fr
2, 3
E♭7
A♭ 4fr
man. Then she
wine, and I was al -
band, and I was al -
A♭7 4fr
D♭
most per - suad - ed to
most per - suad - ed to

A♭
4fr
E♭
3fr
strip my-self of my pride.
let strange lips lead me on.
A♭
A♭7
D♭
Al - most persuad - ed to
Al - most persuad - ed but your
1
D.S.
A♭
E♭7
push my con - science a - side. Then we
2
D♭
sweet love made me stop and go home.

ALWAYS ON MY MIND

Words and Music by WAYNE THOMPSON,
MARK JAMES and JOHNNY CHRISTOPHER

Slow Ballad

F C7

mf

F C/E Dm F/C

May-be I did-n't treat you __ quite as good _ as I
May-be I did-n't hold you __ all those lone-ly, lone-ly

B♭ C F C/E

should have. May-be I did-n't love you __
times, __ and I guess I nev-er told you __

Dm F/C G/B 𝄋 B♭

quite as of-ten as I could have. _ (1.,3.) Lit-tle things I should have
I'm so hap-py that you're mine. _____ (2.) If I made you feel __

F/A Bb F/A Gm 3fr Bb/F Bb/D
said __ and done, I just nev - er took the time. ______
sec - ond best, girl, I'm sor - ry I was blind. ______
To Coda
C7 Dm7 C7/E F Gm 3fr Am Bb C7
You were al - ways on my mind. You were al - ways on my
1 F Bb C7
mind.
2 F Bb C7 F C/E Dm F/C
mind. Tell ______ me,
Bb F/A Gm 3fr C7 F C/E
tell me that your sweet love __ has-n't died. ______ Give ______

Dm
F/C
B♭
F/A
Gm
3fr
C
me, give me one more chance to keep you sat - is - fied, sat - is -
F
D.S. al Coda
fied.
CODA
B♭
You are al-ways on my
C7
F
C/E
Dm
F/C
mind.
B♭
Am
Gm7
C7
F
You are al-ways on my mind.
rit.

BEFORE HE CHEATS

Words and Music by JOSH KEAR
and CHRIS TOMPKINS

D
C♯7
F♯m
fruit - y lit - tle drink 'cause she can't shoot whis - key. Right now, he's
and he's a - think - ing that he's gon - na get luck - y. Right now, he's
E
D
C♯7
prob - 'ly up be - hind her with a pool stick, show - ing her how to shoot a com - bo.
prob - 'ly dab - bing on three dol - lar's worth of that bath - room co - logne.
B7
C♯
And he don't know I
Oh, and he don't know that I
D
F♯m
D
F♯m
dug my key in - to the side of his pret - ty lit - tle souped - up four - wheel drive,

D
F♯m
C♯
carved my name in - to his leath - er seat.
I took a
D
F♯m
D
F♯m
To Coda
Lou - is - ville Slug - ger to both head - lights,
slashed a hole in all four tires,
and
D
1
C♯
F♯m
E
may - be next time he'll think be - fore he cheats.
D
C♯7
2
C♯
F♯m
be - fore he cheats.

A
E
D
I might have saved a lit - tle trou - ble for the next girl,
B
C
C♯
'cause the next time that he cheats,
oh, you know
F♯m
E
D
it won't be on me.
No,
C♯
F♯m
C♯m/E
4fr
D
not on me.

C♯
D.S. al Coda
'Cause I
CODA
D
C♯
B
may-be next time he'll think before he cheats.
A/C♯
D
C♯
Oh, may-be next time he'll think be-fore he
F♯m
E
D
E
cheats. Oh, be-fore he
F♯m
E
D
C♯
cheats. Oh...
rall.

BEHIND CLOSED DOORS

Words and Music by
KENNY O'DELL

G D/A G7 C
crowd. 'Cause peo - ple like to talk,
want you." She's al - ways a la - dy,
F F/G C
Lord, don't they love to talk. But when they
just like a la - dy should be. But when they
Dm F G7
turn out the lights, I know she'll be leav - in' with
turn out the lights, she's still a ba - by to
C F G7
me. And when we get be - hind closed
me.
3

C F G7 C
doors, then she lets her hair hang down, and she makes me
F Em Dm Dm7 G
glad I'm a man. Oh, no one knows what
Dm7 G7 C
goes on be - hind closed doors.
1 G7
My
2 F G9 9fr C
Be - hind closed doors.
3
3

BLESS THE BROKEN ROAD

Words and Music by MARCUS HUMMON,
BOBBY BOYD and JEFF HANNA

Am7 G F C/E Dm7 G7sus
I got lost a time or two, wiped my brow and kept push-in' through.
C/E Fsus2 G Am F F/G C
I could-n't see how ev-er-y sign point-ed straight to you.
Dm C/E F6 C/F 3fr C Dm C/E G G7 C
But ev-er-y long lost dream led me to where you are.
Dm C/E F C/F 3fr Am7 G/B C Dm7 C
Oth-ers who broke my heart, they were like north-ern stars

G C Dm C/E F C/F C Dm C/E G G7 Am
3fr
pointing me on my way into your loving arms.
G/B C Dm7 C/E Fsus2 C/F
3
This much I know is true: that
To Coda
C/E F G Am F F/G C/E Fsus2
God blessed the broken road that led me straight to you.
G Am F F/G C/G C C/E Fsus2
Yes, He did.

G Am7 F F/G C/G C C/E Fsus2
I think a - bout the years
G Am F G C C/E Fsus2
I've spent just pass - in' through. I'd like to have the time
G Am F F/G C Am11 3fr
I lost and give it back to you. But you just smile and take
G F C/E Dm7 F/G C/E Fsus2
my hand. You've been there, you un - der - stand it's all part of a grand -

D.S. al Coda
G
Am
F
F/G
C
Dm
C/E
- er plan __ that is com - in' true. ______ Ev - er - y
CODA
N.C.
F/C
C
F(add9)
C
G
C
F
Am
Dm
C
G/B
C
F
F(add9)
C
Now I'm just a - roll - in' __ home __

G Am G/B C
in - to my lov - er's arms. This much I
Dm7 C/E Fsus2 C/F C/E Fsus2
3fr
know is true: that God blessed the bro -
G Am F F/G C/E Fsus2
- ken road that led me straight to you,
G Am F F/G C/G C C/E Fsus2
that God blessed the bro -

G
Am
F
G
- ken road
that led me straight
C/E
Fsus2
G
Am
to you.
F
F/G
C/G
C
C/E
Fsus2
G
Am
rit.
F
F/G
C

A BOY NAMED SUE

Words and Music by
SHEL SILVERSTEIN

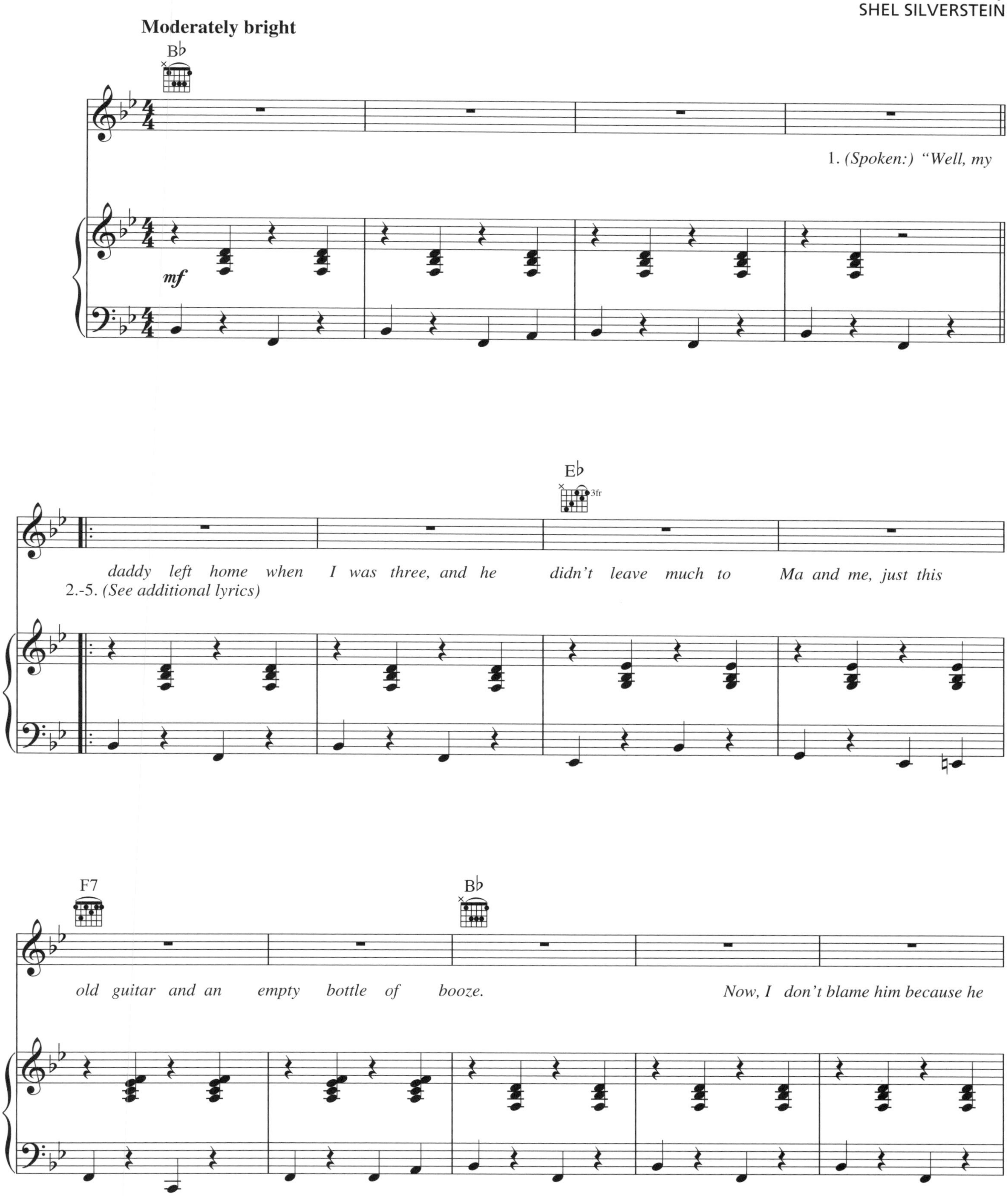
Moderately bright
B♭
1. (Spoken:) "Well, my
mf
daddy left home when I was three, and he didn't leave much to Ma and me, just this
2.-5. (See additional lyrics)
E♭
3fr
F7
B♭
old guitar and an empty bottle of booze.
Now, I don't blame him because he

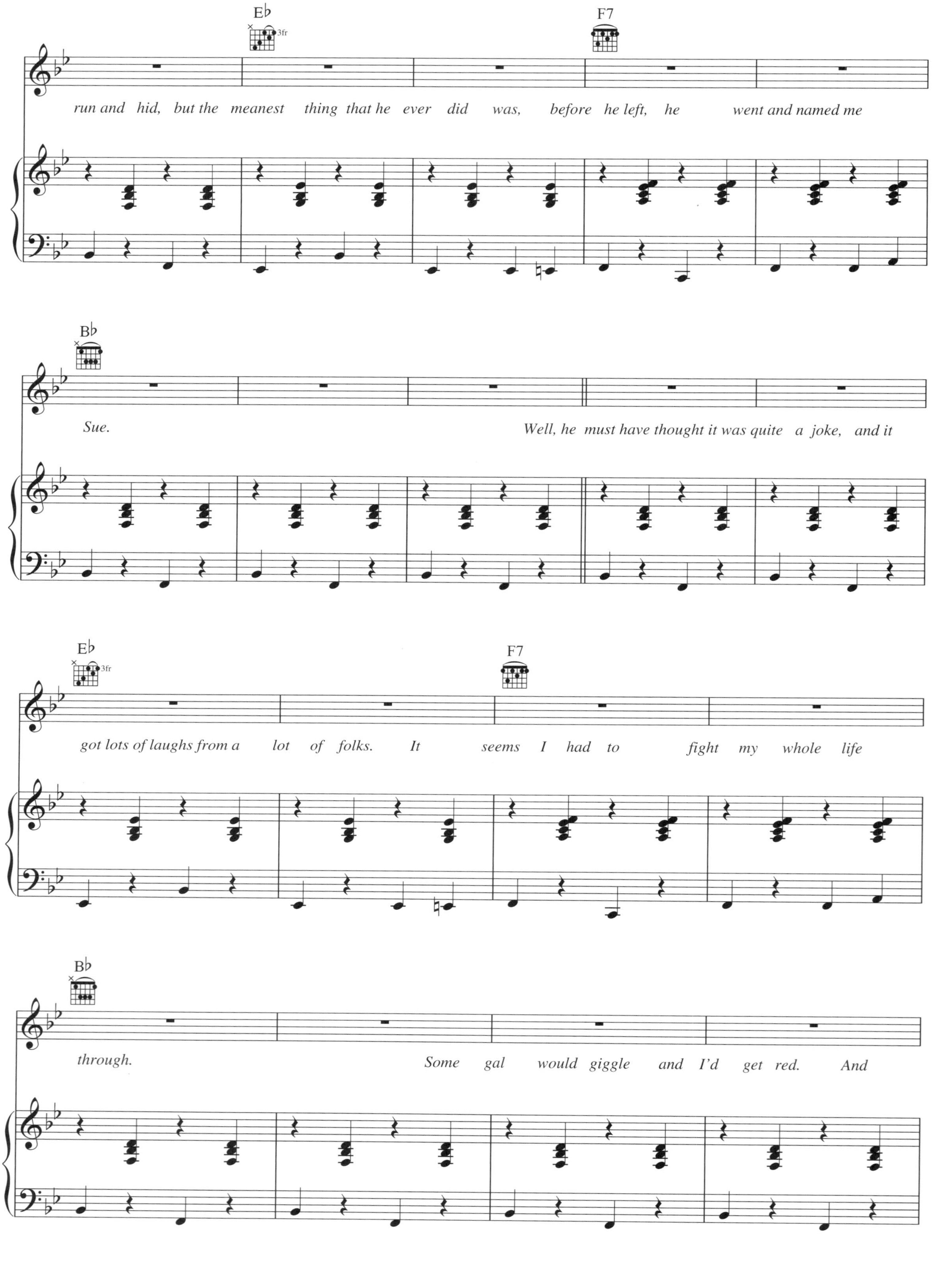
E♭
3fr
F7
run and hid, but the meanest thing that he ever did was, before he left, he went and named me
B♭
Sue.
Well, he must have thought it was quite a joke, and it
E♭
3fr
F7
got lots of laughs from a lot of folks. It seems I had to fight my whole life
B♭
through.
Some gal would giggle and I'd get red. And

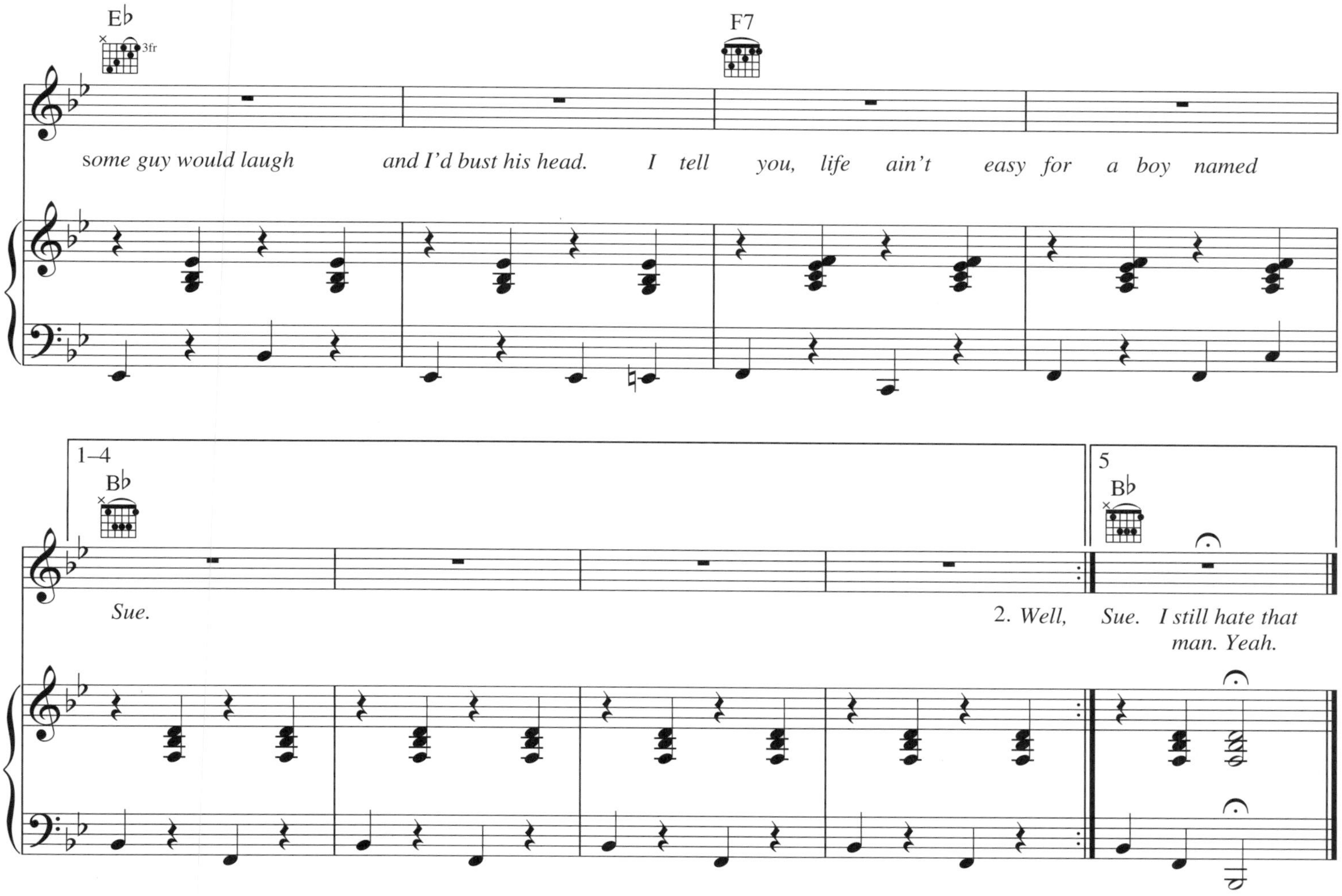
E♭
3fr
F7
some guy would laugh and I'd bust his head. I tell you, life ain't easy for a boy named
1–4
B♭
Sue.
2. Well,
5
B♭
Sue. I still hate that
man. Yeah.

Additional Lyrics

2. *Well, I grew up quick and I grew up mean;*
My fists got hard and my wits got keen.
Roamed from town to town to hide my shame,
But I made me a vow to the moon and stars,
I'd search the honky-tonks and bars,
And kill that man that give me that awful name.

Well, it was Gatlinburg in mid July,
And I had just hit town and my throat was dry.
I'd thought I'd stop and have myself a brew.
At an old saloon on a street of mud,
There at a table dealin' stud,
Sat the dirty, mangy dog that named me Sue.

3. *Well, I knew that snake was my own sweet dad*
From a worn-out picture that my mother had.
And I knew that scar on his cheek and his evil eye.
He was big and bent and gray and old,
And I looked at him and my blood ran cold,
And I said, "My name is Sue. How do you do?
Now you gonna die." Yeah, that's what I told him.

Well, I hit him hard right between the eyes,
And he went down, but to my surprise
He come up with a knife and cut off a piece of my ear.
But I busted a chair right across his teeth.
And we crashed through the wall and into the street,
Kickin' and a-gougin' in the mud and the blood and the beer.

4. *I tell you, I've fought tougher men,*
But I really can't remember when.
He kicked like a mule and he bit like a crocodile.
I heard him laugh and then I heard him cussin';
He went for his gun and I pulled mine first.
He stood there lookin' at me and I saw him smile.

And he said, "Son, this world is rough,
And if a man's gonna make it, he's gotta be tough.
And I know I wouldn't be there to help you along.
So I give you that name and I said, 'Goodbye.'
I knew you'd have to get tough or die.
And it's that name that helped to make you strong."

5. *Yeah, he said, "Now you just fought one helluva fight,*
And I know you hate me and you've got the right
To kill me now and I wouldn't blame you if you do.
But you ought to thank me before I die
For the gravel in your guts and the spit in your eye,
'Cause I'm the ____ that named you Sue."
Yeah, what could I do? What could I do?

I got all choked up and I threw down my gun,
Called him my pa and he called me his son.
And I come away with a different point of view.
And I think about him now and then,
Ev'ry time I try and ev'ry time I win.
And if I ever have a son, I think I'm gonna name him...
Bill or George. Anything but Sue.
I still hate that man. Yeah.

BLUE

Words and Music by
BILL MACK

A
C♯7
F♯9
3fr
Blue, oh, so
Instrumental solo
B7
E7
lone - some for you. Tears fill my eyes till I can't
A
D
A
N.C.
C♯7
see. Three o' - clock in the morn -
Solo ends
Now that it's o -
F♯7
- ing here am I
- ver, I re - al - ized

B7
E7
To Coda
sit - ting here so lone - ly, so lone-some I could
those weak words you whis-pered were noth-ing but
D/F♯ E7/G♯ A C♯7
cry. Blue,
F♯9
3fr
oh, so lone-some for you. Why can't you be
B7
D.S. al Coda
E7 A E7 D7/F♯ E7/G♯
blue o - ver me?

CODA
F7
B♭
D7
lies.
Blue,
G9
9fr
C7
oh, so lone-some for you.
Why can't you be
F7
B♭
A
B♭
B
C7
blue o-ver me?
Why can't you be
F7
B♭
blue o - ver me?
rit.

BROKEN LADY

Words and Music by
LARRY GATLIN

Moderately
G
C
She's a bro - ken la - dy,
mf
G
C
G
wait - ing to be mend - ed, like a pot - ter would
C
G
F
C
mend a bro - ken vase. A

G C G
bro - ken la - dy, wait - ing to be
C G D
To Coda
mend - ed, and have what's left of the piec - es put back in
C G
place. Her love was like a for - tress a-round a man
mp
C G
she would have died for, tak - in' care to take care of all he need - ed;

A
But the la - dy's for - tress slow - ly turned
D
Am7
into a pris - on and the warn - in' signs he gave she nev - er heed -
D7sus4
D7
- ed.
She
G
vowed ev - 'ry morn - in' that what God joined to - geth - er no one

C
G
else in the world could put a - part;
Then the walls came
A
tum - blin' to the ground
and her world came crash - ing down a - round her
Am7
D7
D.S. al Coda
heart.
Now she's a bro -
mf
CODA
C
G
place.
f

BUTTERFLY KISSES

Words and Music by BOB CARLISLE
and RANDY THOMAS

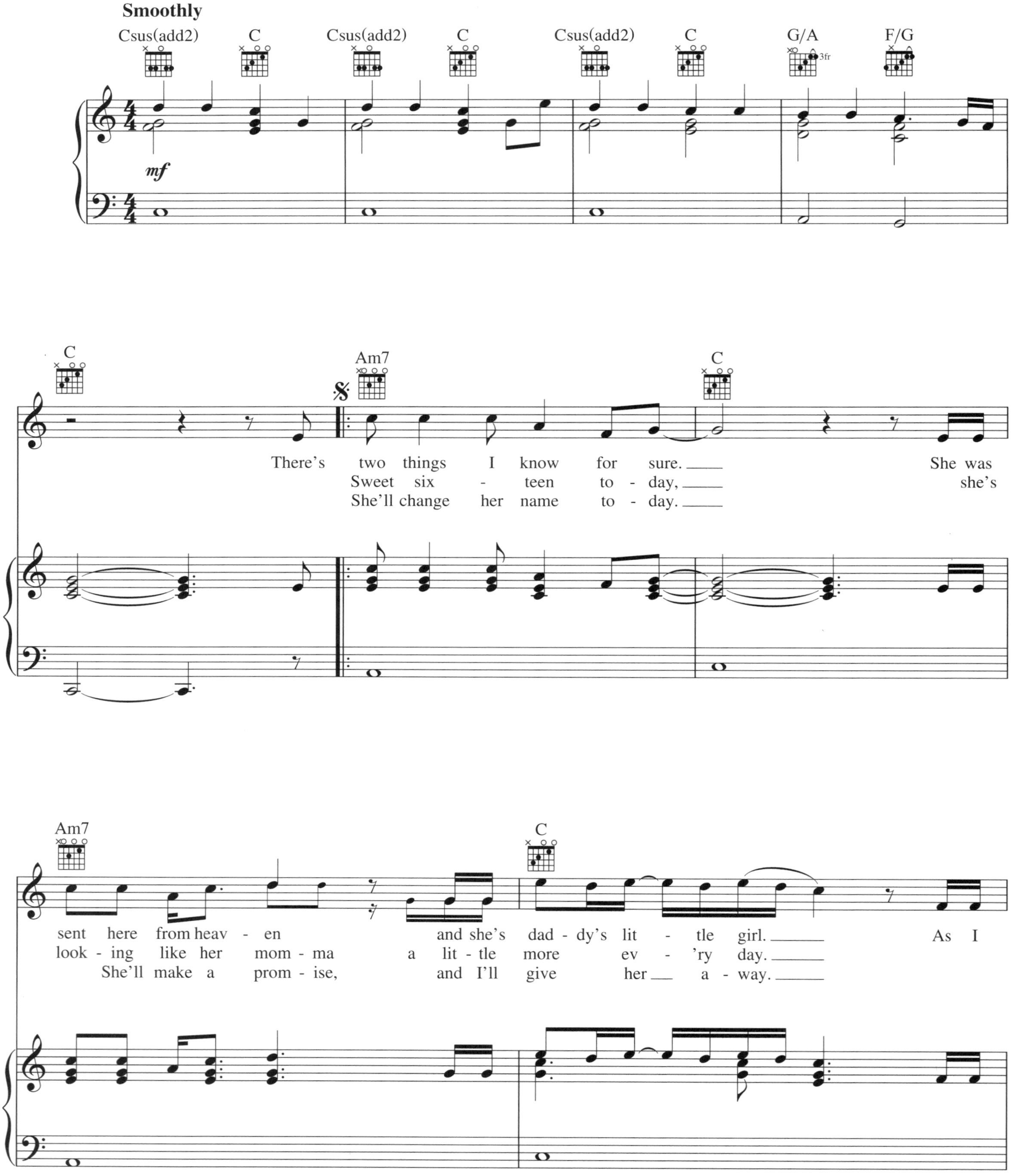
Smoothly
Csus(add2) C Csus(add2) C Csus(add2) C G/A F/G
mf
C Am7 C
There's two things I know for sure. She was
Sweet six - teen to - day, she's
She'll change her name to - day.
Am7 C
sent here from heav - en and she's dad - dy's lit - tle girl. As I
look - ing like her mom - ma a lit - tle more ev - 'ry day.
She'll make a prom - ise, and I'll give her a - way.

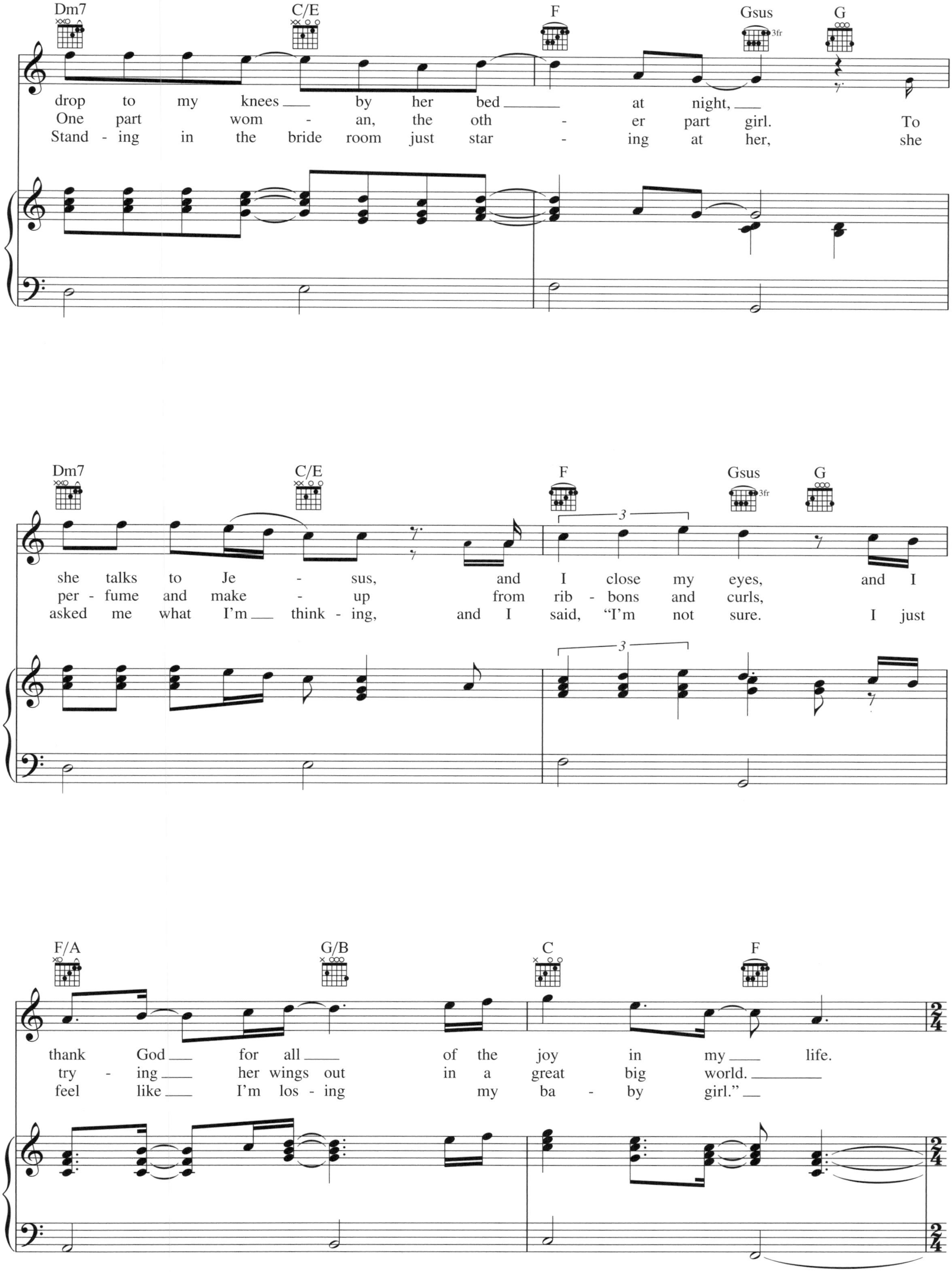
Dm7
C/E
F
Gsus
3fr
G
drop to my knees __ by her bed ______ at night, __
One part wom - an, the oth - er part girl. To
Stand - ing in the bride room just star - ing at her, she
Dm7
C/E
F
Gsus
3fr
G
3
she talks to Je - sus, and I close my eyes, and I
per - fume and make - up from rib - bons and curls,
asked me what I'm __ think - ing, and I said, "I'm not sure. I just
3
F/A
G/B
C
F
thank God __ for all __ of the joy in my __ life.
try - ing __ her wings out in a great big world. ______
feel like __ I'm los - ing my ba - by girl." __

G7sus
Csus(add2)
C
Oh, but most of all, for but - ter - fly kiss - es af - ter
But I re - mem - ber but - ter - fly kiss - es af - ter
Then she leaned o - ver, gave me but - ter - fly kiss - es with her
Csus(add2)
C
Csus(add2)
C
Csus(add2)
bed - time prayer, stick - in' lit - tle white flow - ers all up in her
bed - time prayer, stick - in' lit - tle white flow - ers all up in her
mom - ma there, stick - in' lit - tle white flow - ers all up in her
Am
G
F
hair. "Walk be - side the po - ny, Dad - dy, it's
hair. "You know how much I love you, Dad - dy, but if
hair. "Walk me down the aisle, Dad - dy, it's
C/E
F
my first ride. I know the cake looks fun - ny, Dad - dy, but
you don't mind, I'm on - ly goin' to kiss you on the
just a - bout time. Does my wed - ding gown look pret - ty, Dad - dy? Dad -

C/E
F/A
G/B
I sure tried." Oh, with all that I've done wrong, I must have done
cheek this time."
dy, don't cry."
C
D7sus
D7
some - thing right to de - serve a
her
her
rit.
To Coda
F
G5
3fr
Csus(add2)
C
hug ev-'ry morn - ing and but - ter - fly kiss - es at night.
love
love
a tempo
1
Csus(add2)
C
Csus(add2)
C
G/A
3fr
F/G
C(add2)

2
Csus(add2)
C
E♭
G7sus/D
(All the pre - cious time.)
Like the
Csus(add2)
C
Csus(add2)
C
wind, the years go by.
(Pre - cious but - ter -
E♭
G7sus/D
F/A
Dm7
G7
D.S. al Coda
fly, spread your wings and fly.)
CODA
G7sus
F/A
but - ter - fly kiss - es. I could - n't ask God for more. Man,

G/B
A♭maj7
this is what love is. I know I've got-ta let her go, but I'll
C/G
F
al - ways re-mem - ber ev - 'ry hug in the morn - ing and
molto rit.
a tempo
G7sus
Csus(add2)
C
Csus(add2)
C
but - ter - fly kiss - es.
Csus(add2)
C
G/A
3fr
F/G
C
molto rit.

CITY OF NEW ORLEANS

Words and Music by
STEVE GOODMAN

Moderately bright country tempo
G
D
G
1. Rid - in' on the Cit - y of New Or - leans,
2., 3. (See additional lyrics)
Em
C
Il - li - nois Cen - tral Mon - day morn - in' rail.
G
D
Fif-teen cars and fif - teen rest - less rid -

G
Em
D
- ers, three con - duc - tors and twen - ty - five sacks of mail; _
G
Em
_ All a - long the south - bound
Bm
Od - y - ssey, _ the train pulls out of Kan - ka - kee _ and
D
A
rolls a - long _ the hous - es, farms _ and fields. _

Em
Pass - in' towns that have no name and
Bm
D
freight - yards full of old black men, and the grave - yards of the
D7
G
Am
Bm
rust - ed au - to - mo - biles.
C
D7
G
1. Good morn - ing A - mer - i - ca, how are you? Say
2. Good morn - ing A - mer - i - ca, how are you? Said
3. Good night, A - mer - i - ca, how are you? Said

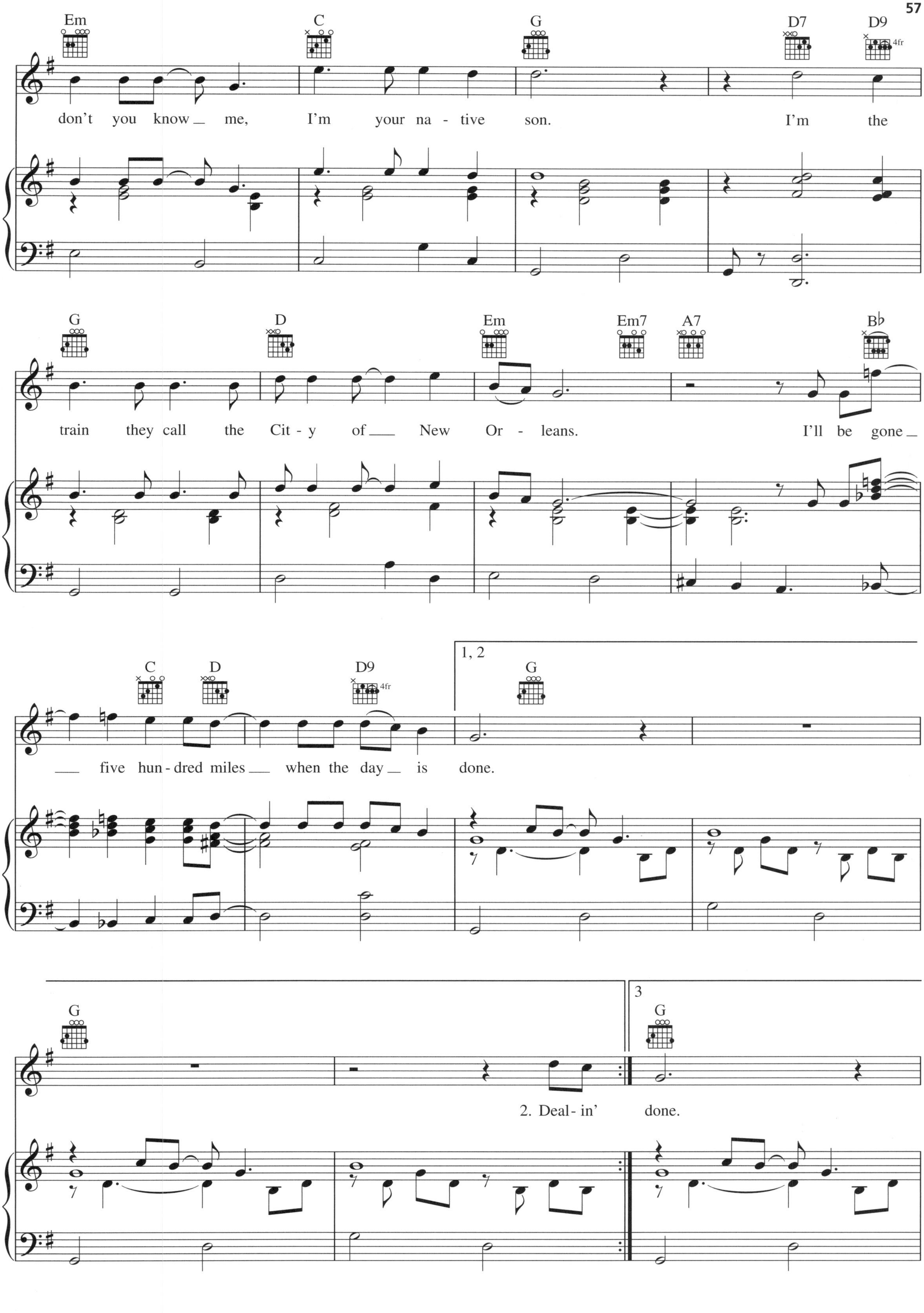
Em C G D7 D9 4fr
don't you know me, I'm your na - tive son. I'm the
G D Em Em7 A7 B♭
train they call the Cit - y of New Or - leans. I'll be gone
C D D9 4fr
1, 2
G
five hun - dred miles when the day is done.
G
3
G
2. Deal - in' done.

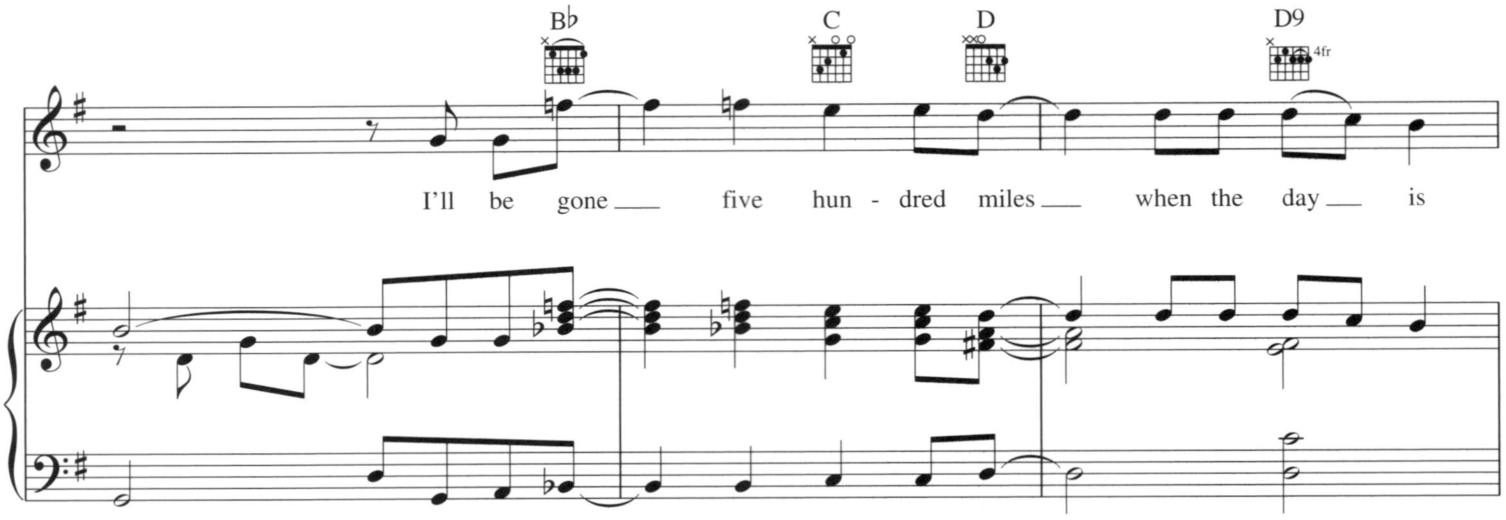

Additional Lyrics

2. Dealin' card games with the old men in the club car,
   Penny a point ain't no one keepin' score.
   Pass the paper bag that holds the bottle;
   Feel the wheels grumblin' 'neath the floor;
   And the sons of Pullman porters, and the sons of engineers
   Ride their father's magic carpet made of steel.
   Mothers with their babes asleep are rockin' to the gentle beat
   And the rhythm of the rails is all they feel.

3. Night time on the City of New Orleans,
   Changin' cars in Memphis, Tennessee;
   Halfway home, we'll be there by mornin',
   Thru the Mississippi darkness rollin' down to the sea.
   But all the towns and people seem to fade into a bad dream,
   And the steel rail still ain't heard the news;
   The conductor sings his songs again;
   The passengers will please refrain,
   This train's got the disappearin' railroad blues.

DON'T IT MAKE MY BROWN EYES BLUE

Words and Music by
RICHARD LEIGH

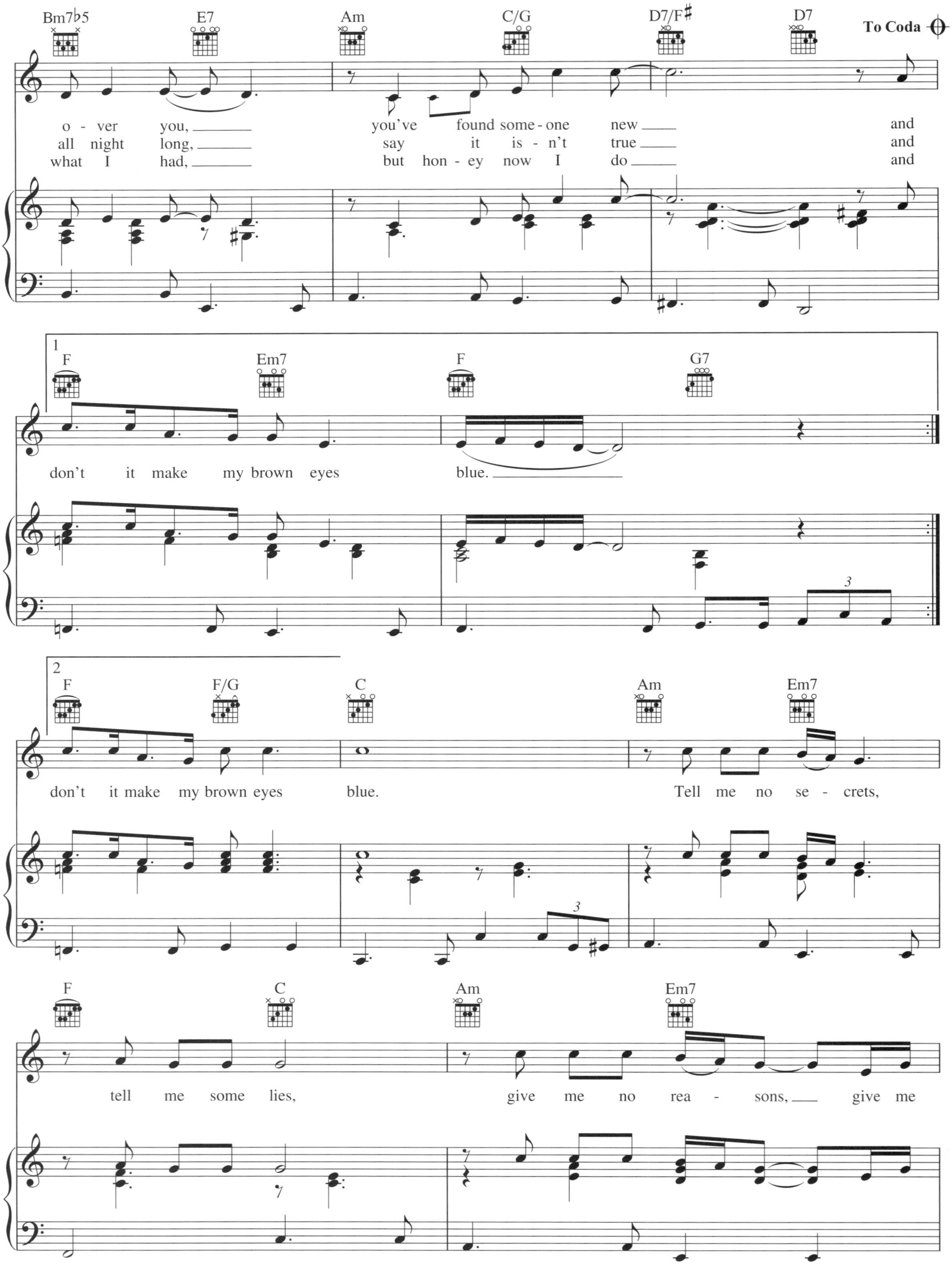
Bm7♭5 E7 Am C/G D7/F♯ D7
To Coda
o - ver you, you've found some - one new and
all night long, say it is - n't true and
what I had, but hon - ey now I do and
1
F Em7 F G7
don't it make my brown eyes blue.
2
F F/G C Am Em7
don't it make my brown eyes blue. Tell me no se - crets,
F C Am Em7
tell me some lies, give me no rea - sons, give me

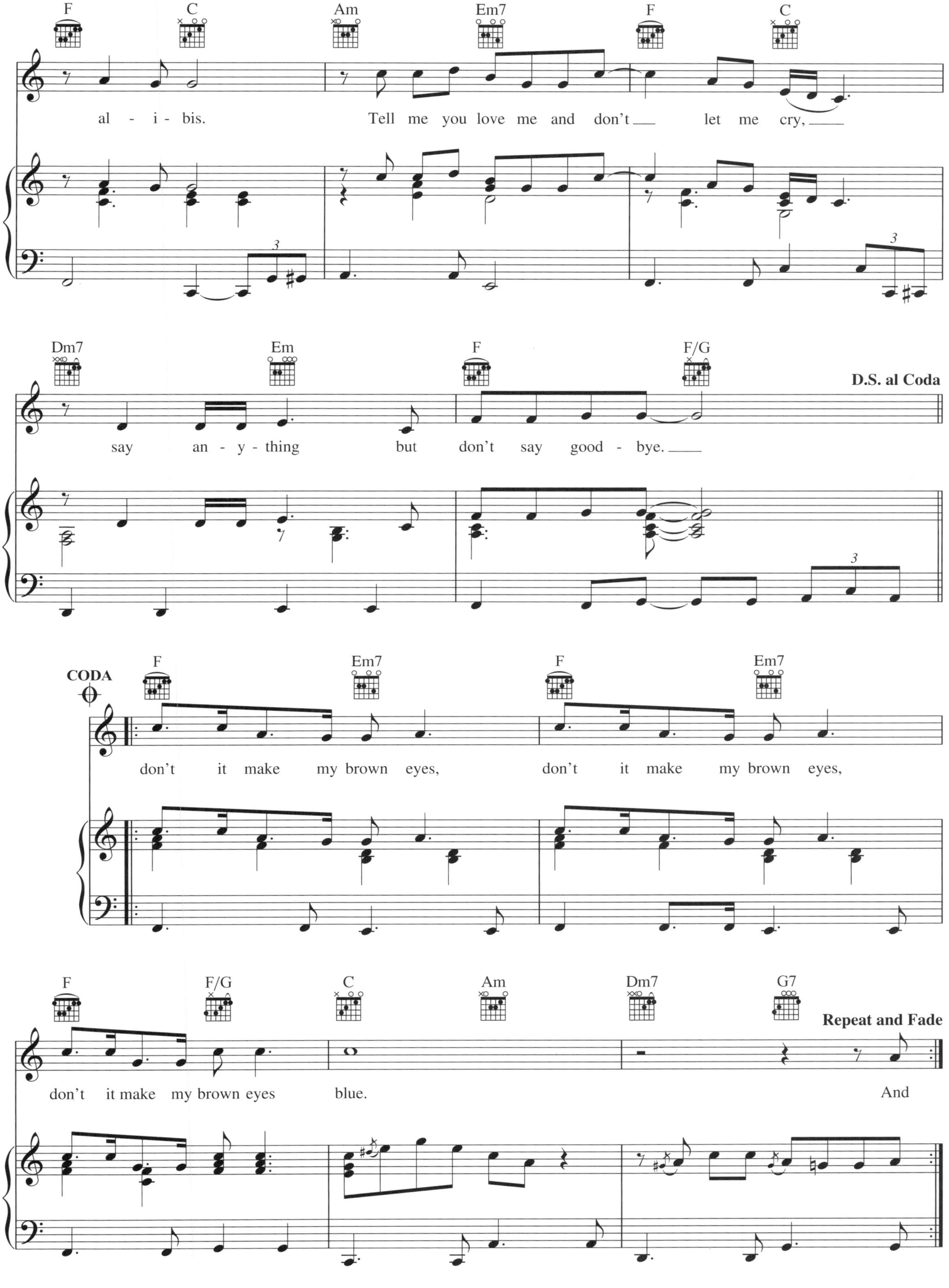
F C Am Em7 F C
al - i - bis. Tell me you love me and don't let me cry,
Dm7 Em F F/G
D.S. al Coda
say an - y - thing but don't say good - bye.
CODA
F Em7 F Em7
don't it make my brown eyes, don't it make my brown eyes,
F F/G C Am Dm7 G7
Repeat and Fade
don't it make my brown eyes blue. And

COME ON OVER

Words and Music by SHANIA TWAIN
and R.J. LANGE

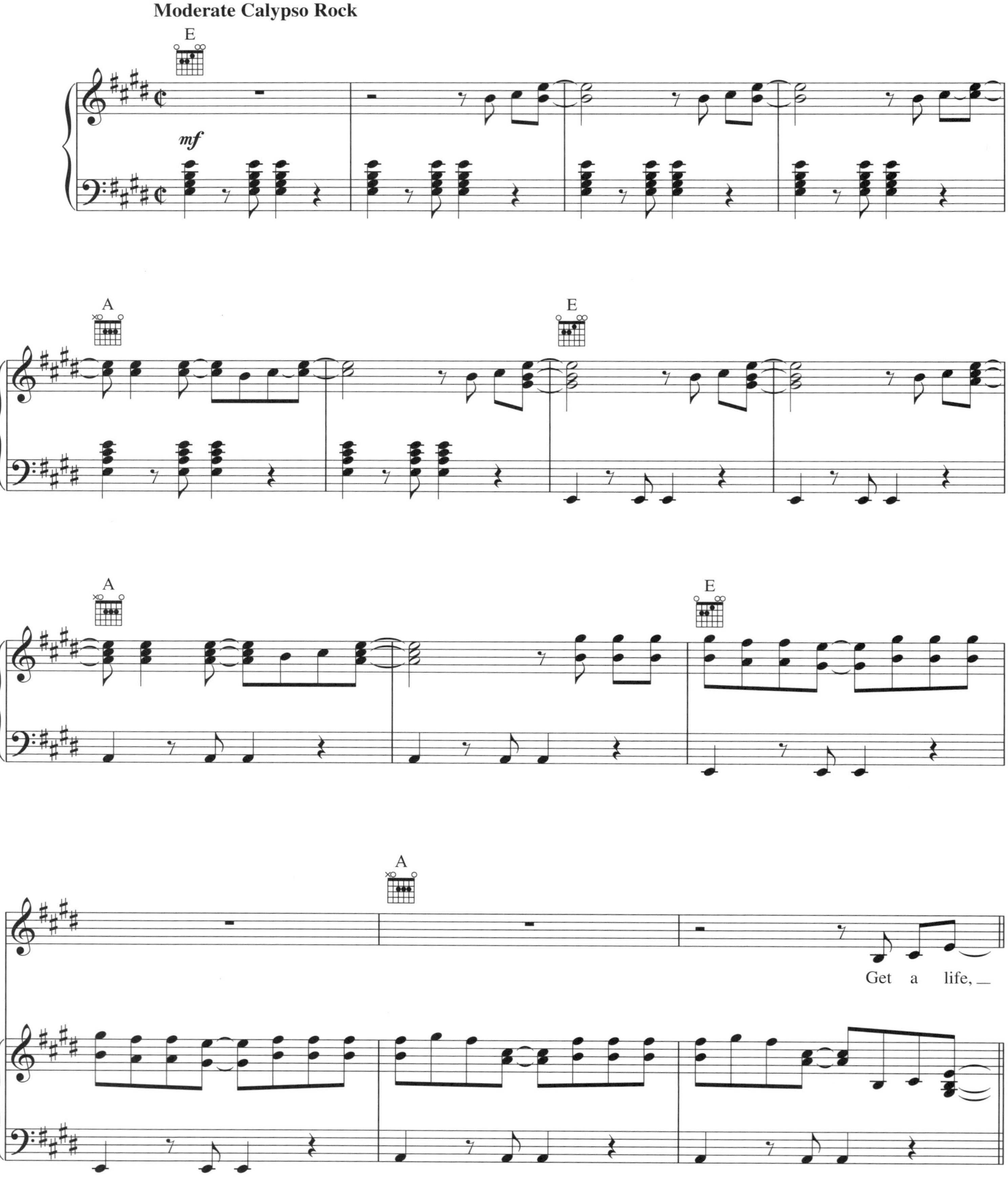

E
A
get a grip, get a - way some - where, take a trip.
E
Take a break, take con - trol, take ad - vice
A
E
from some - one you know. Come on o - ver,
A
come on in; pull up a seat, take a load off your feet.

E
A
Come on o - ver, come on in; you can un - wind, take a
F
load off your mind. Make a wish, make a move, make up
B♭
F
your mind, you can choose. When you're up, when you're down,
B♭
when you need a laugh, come a - round.

F
Bb
Come on o - ver, come on in; pull up a seat, take a
F
load off your feet. Come on o - ver, come on in;
Bb
F
you can un - wind, take a load off your mind. Oh,
Bb
oh.

F
B♭
Oh,
oh.
F♯
Be a win - ner, be a star, yeah, be hap -
get a grip, get a - way
B
- py to be who you are.
some - where, take a trip.
Got - ta be
Take a break,
F♯
your - self, got - ta make a plan, got - ta go
take con - trol, take ad - vise

B
F♯
for it while you can, yeah.
from some - one you know.
Come on o - ver,
B
come on in; pull up a seat, take a load off your feet.
F♯
B
To Coda
Come on o - ver, come on in; you can un - wind, take a
F♯
load off your mind.

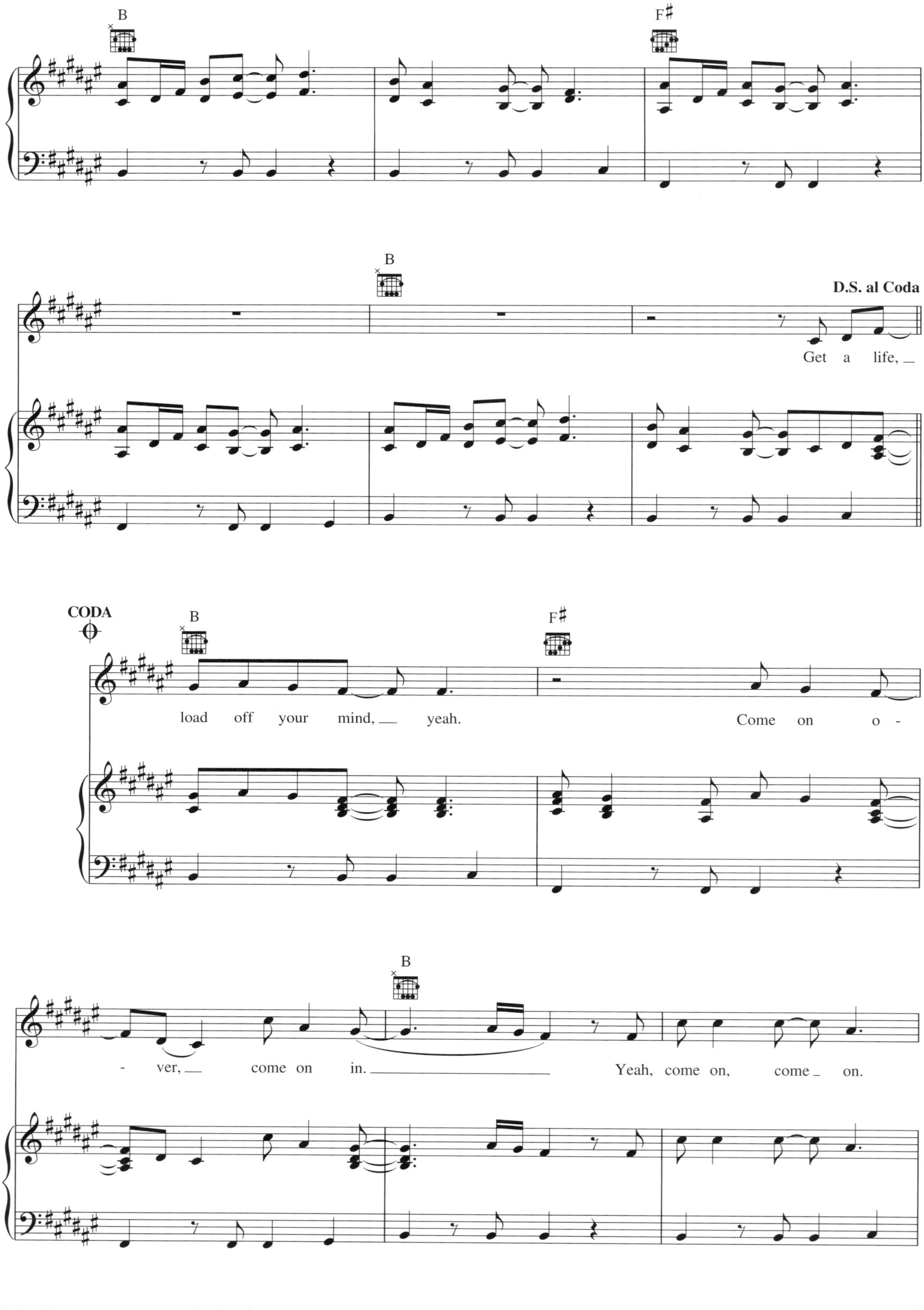
B
F♯
B
D.S. al Coda
Get a life,
CODA
B
F♯
load off your mind, yeah.
Come on o -
B
- ver, come on in.
Yeah, come on, come on.

F♯
B
Oh,
oh.
N.C.
Oh,
B
F♯
oh.
Oh,
B
N.C.
oh,
come on in.

DANG ME

Words and Music by
ROGER MILLER

Moderately fast
F
mf
B♭
C
F
C7
F
B♭
C7
F
(Spoken:) Well,
here I sit high gettin' ideas, ain't nothin' but a fool would live like this.
sittin' 'round drinkin' with the rest of the guys, six rounds bought and I bought five.
roses are red and violets are purple, sugar's sweet and so is maple syrupple, well
B♭
C7
F
Out all night and runnin' wild, my wom-an sit-tin' home with a month-old child.
Spent the groceries and half the rent, I lack four-teen dol-lars hav-in' twen-ty sev-en cents.
I'm the seventh out of seven sons, my pap-py was a pis-tol, I'm a son-of-a-gun.

B♭
C7
F
Dang me, dang me, they ought-ta take a rope and hang me
F7
B♭
N.C.
F
To Coda
high from the high-est tree, wom-an, would you weep for me!
1
2
D.S. al Coda
C7
C7
(Spoken:) Just
(Spoken:) They say
CODA
F
F/C
F7
B♭
C7
F

FOREVER AND EVER, AMEN

Words and Music by PAUL OVERSTREET
and DON SCHLITZ

G
You may won - der how I can
Well, hon - ey, I don't care, I ain't in
D
E
prom - ise you now this love that I feel
love with your hair, and if it all fell out,
A
for you al - ways will be. But
well, I'd love you an - y - way. They say
D
G
D
you're not just time that I'm kill - in'.
time can play tricks on a mem - 'ry,

G
I'm no long - er one of those guys.
make peo - ple for - get things they knew.
D
G
As sure as I live,
Well, it's eas - y to see
D
this love that I give is
it's hap - pen - in' to me. I've al -
E7
A
gon - na be yours un - til the day that I die.
read - y for - got - ten ev - 'ry wom - an but you.

D
G
Oh, ba - by,
Oh, dar - lin',
I'm gon - na love you for - ev -
D
G
- er, for - ev - er and ev -
D
- er, a - men, as
G
D
long as old men sit and talk a - bout the weath -

E
- er, as long as old wom - en sit and
A
D
talk a - bout old men. If you won - der how long
G
D
I'll be faith - ful,
I'll be
well, just
G
E7
hap - py to tell you a - gain.
lis - ten to how this song ends.

G A D G
I'm gon - na love you for - ev - er and ev - er, for -
E A7sus D
ev - er and ev - er, a - men.
1
G A D G
E7 A D
They say

2
G A D
I'm gon - na love you for - ev - er and ev -
G E A
- er, for - ev - er and ev - er, for -
Bm G E
ev - er and ev - er, for - ev - er and ev -
Asus D
- er, a - men.

THE GAMBLER

Words and Music by
DON SCHLITZ

Moderate Country 2
E♭
A♭/E♭
E♭
3fr
mp
A♭/E♭
E♭
On a warm sum-mer's eve - nin', on a
"Son, I've made a life out of
A♭/E♭
E♭
train bound for no - where, I met up with the gam -
read - in' peo - ple's fac - es and know - in' what their cards
- bler, we were both too tired to sleep. So
were by the way they held their eyes. And if
B♭

E♭
A♭/E♭
we took turns a - star - in' out the win - dow at the dark -
you don't mind my say - in', I can see you're out of a -
E♭
1
A♭/E♭
E♭
- ness 'til bore - dom o - ver - took us
- ces. For a
B♭
E♭
2
A♭/E♭
E♭
and he be - gan to speak. He said, taste of your whis - key, I'll
B♭
E♭
give you some ad - vice." So I hand - ed him my bot -
3fr

A♭
E♭
-tle and he drank down my last swal - low. Then he bummed a cig -
B♭
E♭
- a - rette and asked me for a light. And the night got death - ly qui -
A♭
E♭
- et, and his face lost all ex - pres - sion, said, "If you're
A♭
E♭
B♭
E♭
gon - na play the game, boy, ya got - ta learn to play it right. You got to
4fr
3fr

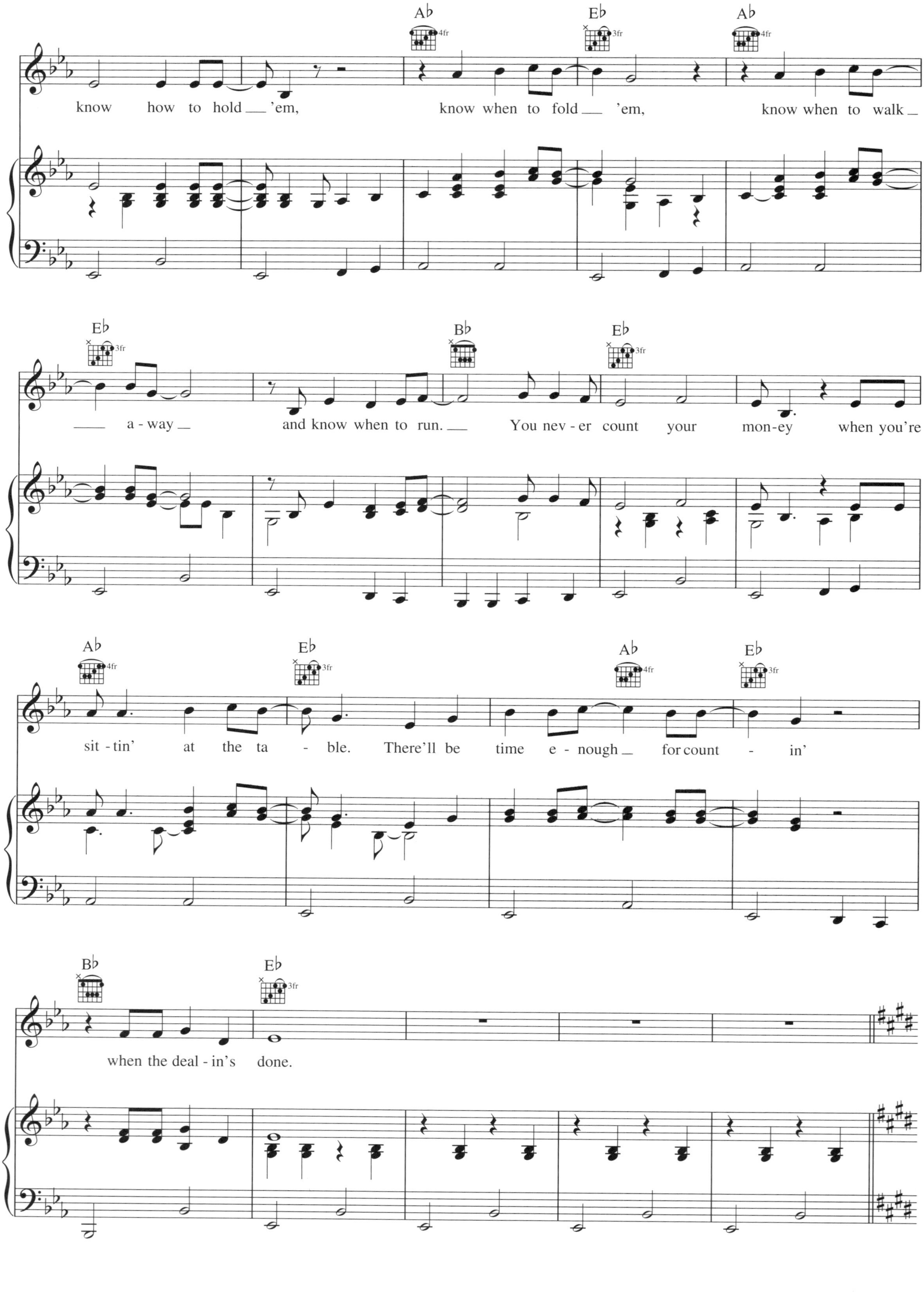
A♭ E♭ A♭
know how to hold ’em, know when to fold ’em, know when to walk
E♭ B♭ E♭
a - way and know when to run. You nev - er count your mon - ey when you’re
A♭ E♭ A♭ E♭
sit - tin’ at the ta - ble. There’ll be time e - nough for count - in’
B♭ E♭
when the deal - in’s done.

E A E
Ev-'ry gam-bler knows that the se-cret to sur-viv-in' is
B
know-in' what to throw a-way and know-in' what to keep. 'Cause
E A E
ev-'ry hand's a win-ner and ev-'ry hand's a los-er and the
A E B E
best that you can hope for is to die in your sleep." And

A E
when he'd fin-ished speak-in', he turned back towards the win - dow,
B
crushed out his cig - a - rette and fad - ed off to sleep. And
E A E
some-where in the dark - ness the gam - bler he broke e - ven but
A E B E
in his fi - nal words I found an ace that I could keep. You got to

E A E A
know when to hold ’em, know when to fold ’em, know when to walk
E B E B9
a - way and know when to run. You nev - er count your
E A E A
mon-ey when you’re sit-tin’ at the ta - ble. There’ll be time e-nough for count -
E B 1 E 2 E
- in’ when the deal - in’s done. You got to done.

GENTLE ON MY MIND

Words and Music by
JOHN HARTFORD

C
couch. And it's
Cmaj7 C6 Cmaj7
know-ing I'm not shack-led by for - got - ten words and bonds_ and the
C Cmaj7 Dm
ink stains that have dried up - on some line
Dm7
that keeps you in the back - roads by the

Additional Lyrics

2. It's not clinging to the rocks and ivy planted on their columns now that binds me,
   Or something that somebody said because they thought we fit together walkin'.
   It's just knowing that the world will not be cursing or forgiving when I walk along
   Some railroad track and find
   That you're moving on the backroads by the rivers of my memory, and for hours
   You're just gentle on my mind.

3. Though the wheat fields and the clotheslines and junkyards and the highways
   Come between us,
   And some other woman crying to her mother 'cause she turned and I was gone.
   I still run in silence, tears of joy might stain my face and summer sun might
   Burn me 'til I'm blind,
   But not to where I cannot see you walkin' on the backroads by the rivers flowing
   Gentle on my mind.

4. I dip my cup of soup back from the gurglin' cracklin' caldron in some train yard,
   My beard a roughening coal pile and a dirty hat pulled low across my face.
   Through cupped hands 'round a tin can I pretend I hold you to my breast and find
   That you're waving from the backroads by the rivers of my memory, ever smilin',
   Ever gentle on my mind.

GO REST HIGH ON THAT MOUNTAIN

Words and Music by
VINCE GILL

D
D/F♯
G
D
pain. You weren't a - fraid to face the dev - il. You're no
A7sus
A7
D
Chorus
stran - ger to the rain. Go rest
D
G
D
D/F♯
high on that moun - tain. Son, your
3
G
D
G
work on earth is done. Go to heav - en a - shout -
3

Additional Lyrics

2. Oh, how we cried the day you left us,
We gathered 'round your grave to grieve.
I wish I could see the angels' faces
When they hear your sweet voice sing.
Chorus

GRANDPA
(Tell Me 'Bout the Good Old Days)

Words and Music by
JAMIE O'HARA

*Melody is written an octave higher than sung.

A
this world's gone cra - zy.
but I just don't know.
And
D
Grand - pa,
Grand - pa,
G
take me back to yes - ter - day,
let's wan - der back in - to the past,
D
when the line be - tween right and wrong
then paint me the pic - ture
A7
D
did - n't seem so haz - y.
of long a - go.

G
Did lov - ers real - ly fall in love to stay
D
and stand be - side each oth - er come what may?
A7
Was a prom - ise real - ly some - thing peo - ple kept,
D
not just some - thing they would say (and then for - get)?

G
Did fam-'lies real-ly bow their heads to pray? Did dad-dys real-ly
D
Em
nev-er go a-way? Oh, oh, Grand-pa, tell
G/A
3fr
1
D
me 'bout the good old days.
2
D
Em
Oh, oh, Grand-pa, tell

G/A
D
3fr
me 'bout the good old days.
G
D
A7
D.S. and Fade
Optional Ending
D
D
Did fam-'lies real - ly

(Hey, Won't You Play)
ANOTHER SOMEBODY DONE SOMEBODY WRONG SONG

Words and Music by LARRY BUTLER
and CHIPS MOMAN

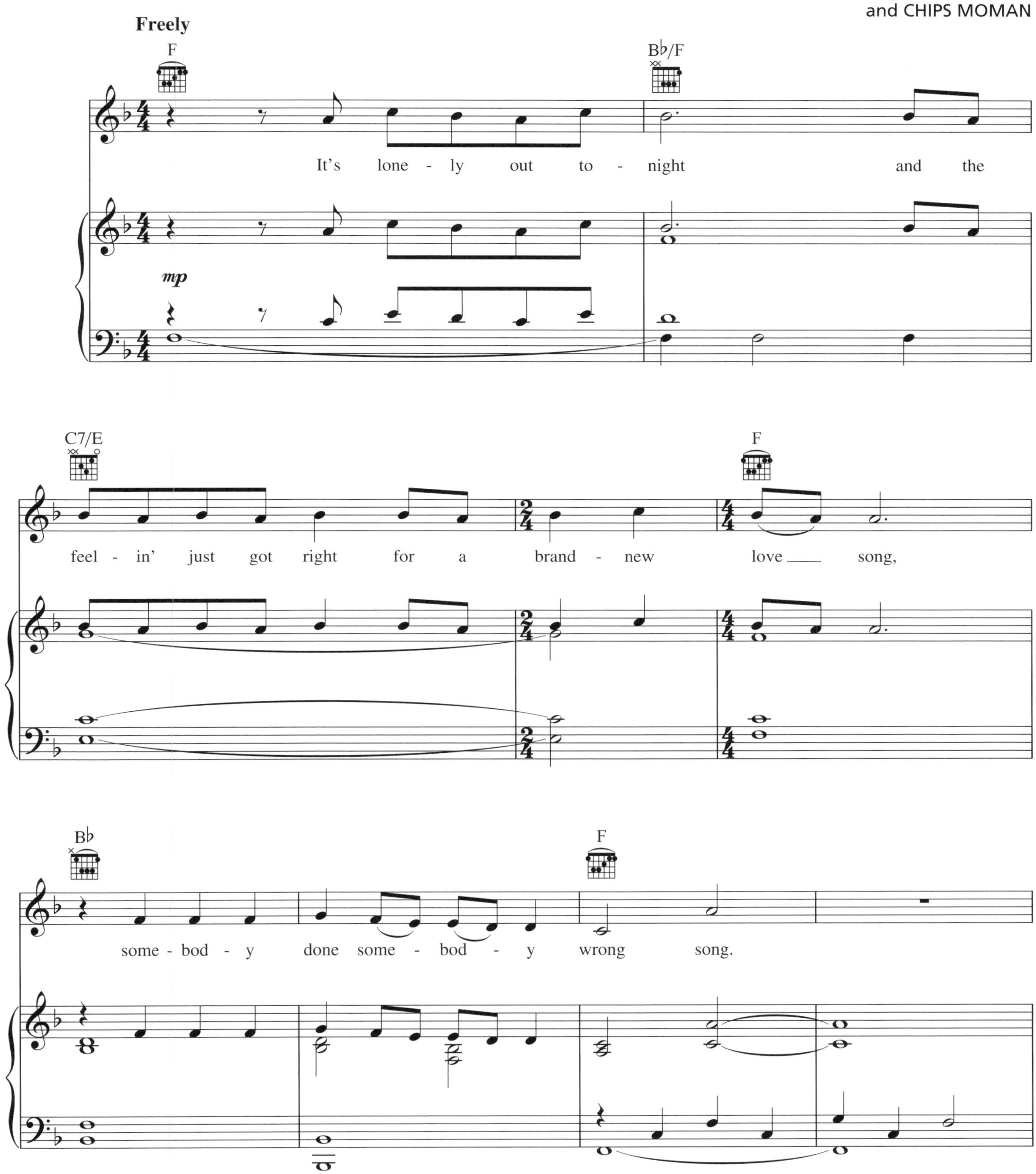

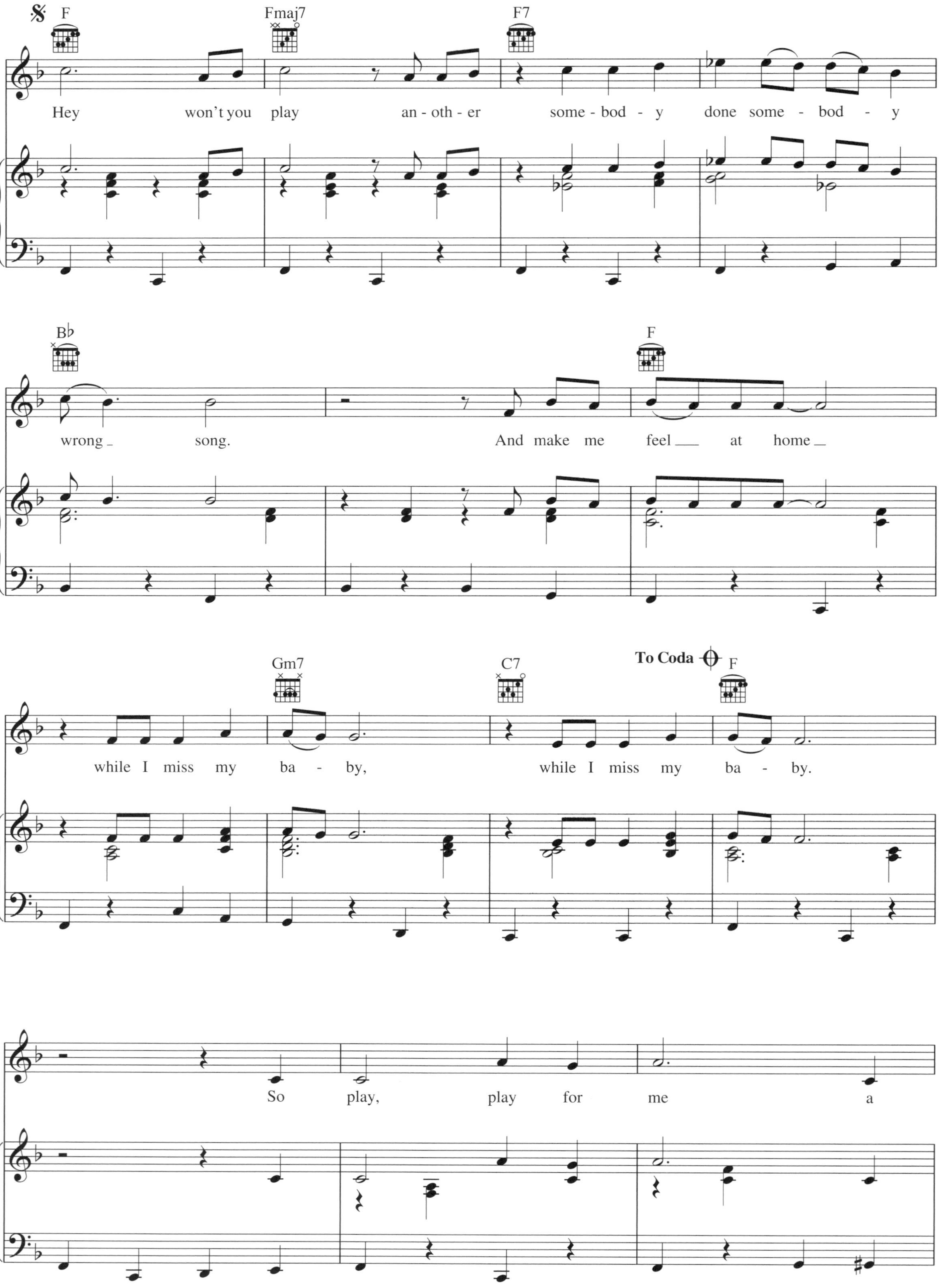
F
Fmaj7
F7
Hey won't you play an - oth - er some - bod - y done some - bod - y
B♭
F
wrong song. And make me feel at home
Gm7
C7
To Coda
F
while I miss my ba - by, while I miss my ba - by.
So play, play for me a

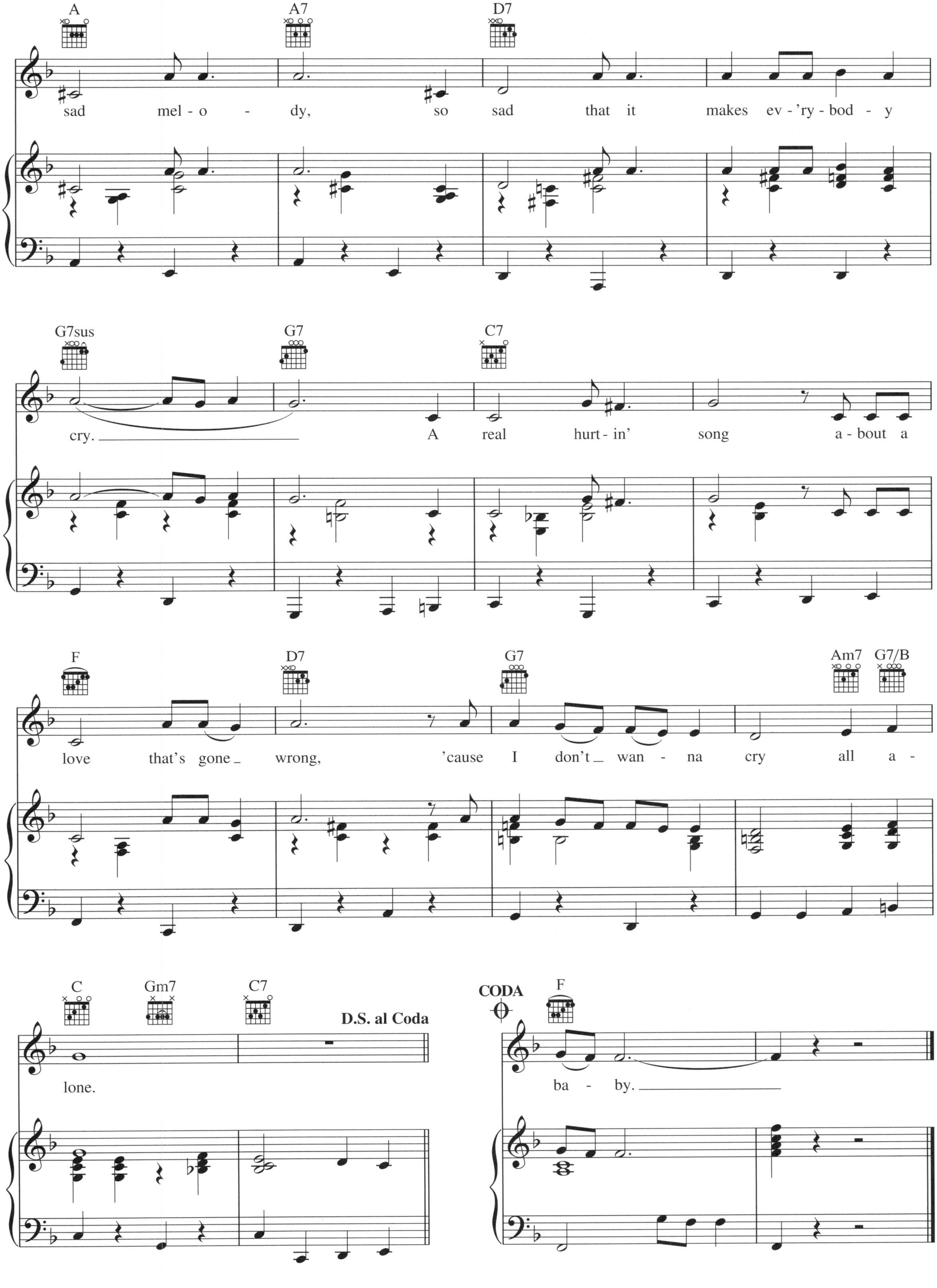
A
A7
D7
sad mel - o - dy, so sad that it makes ev - 'ry - bod - y
G7sus
G7
C7
cry. A real hurt - in' song a - bout a
F
D7
G7
Am7
G7/B
love that's gone wrong, 'cause I don't wan - na cry all a -
C
Gm7
C7
D.S. al Coda
lone.
CODA
F
ba - by.

HELP ME MAKE IT THROUGH THE NIGHT

Words and Music by
KRIS KRISTOFFERSON

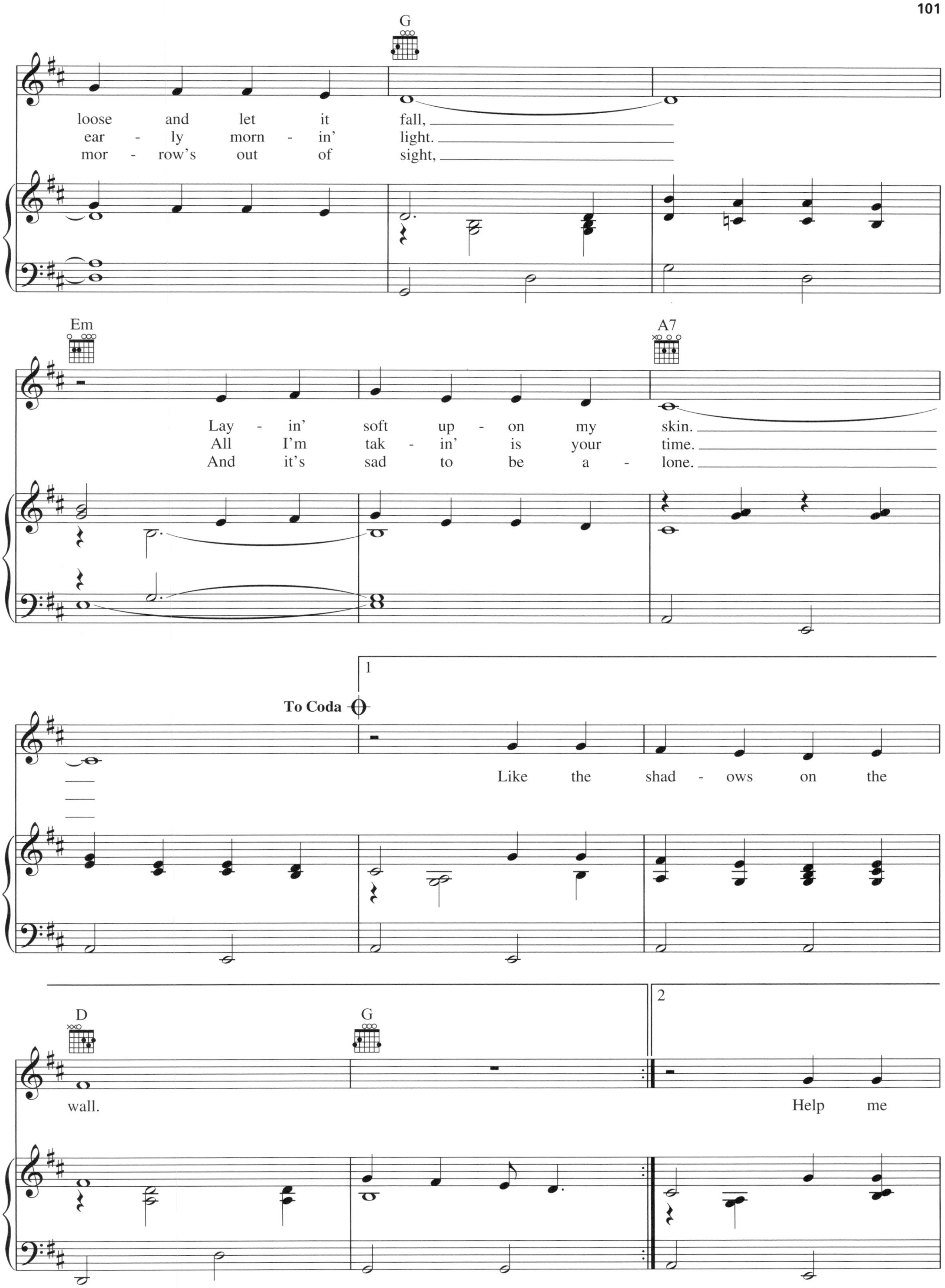
G
loose and let it fall,
ear - ly morn - in' light.
mor - row's out of sight,
Em
A7
Lay - in' soft up - on my skin.
All I'm tak - in' is your time.
And it's sad to be a - lone.
To Coda
1
Like the shad - ows on the
D
G
wall.
2
Help me

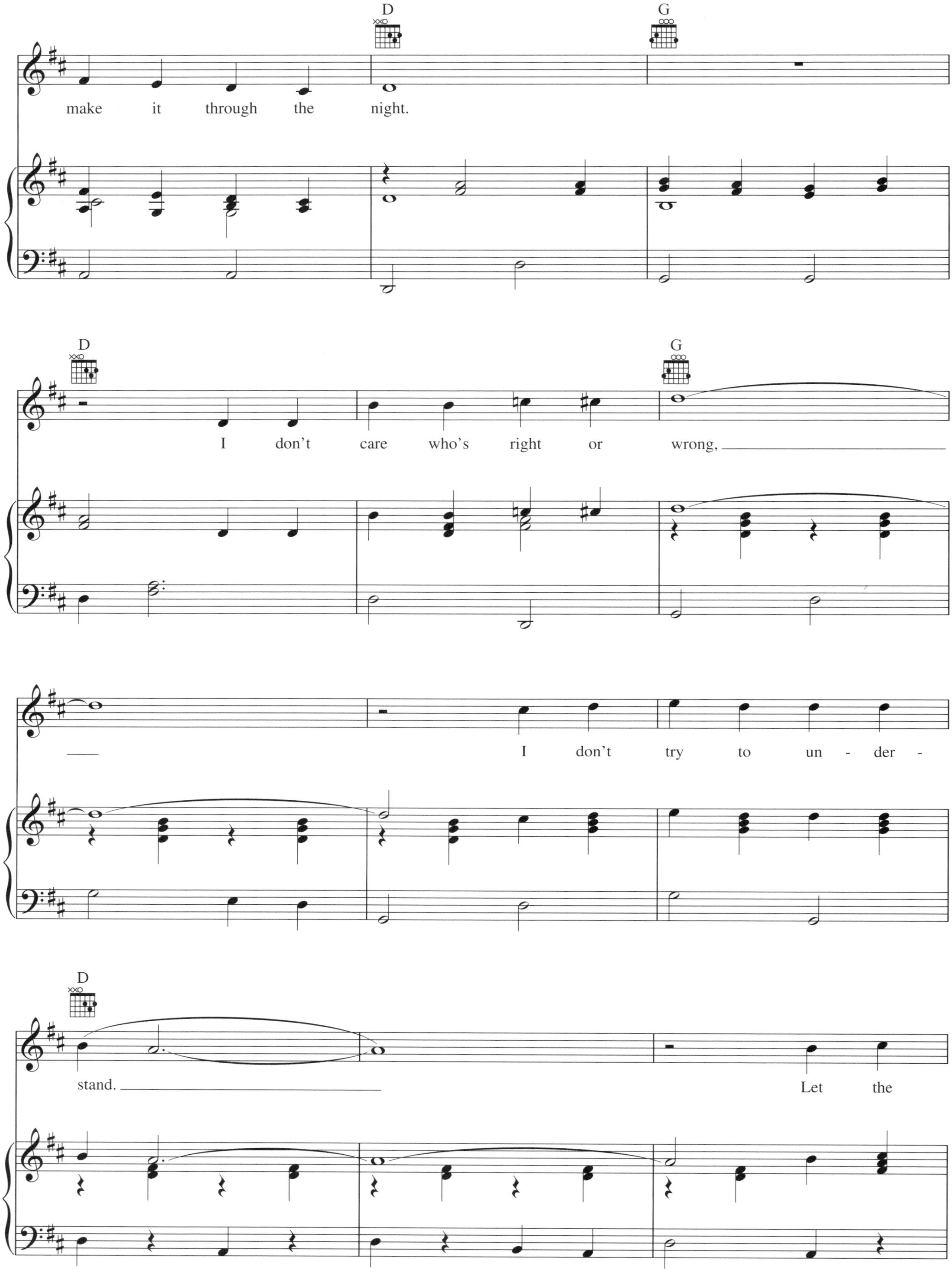
D
G
make it through the night.
D
G
I don't care who's right or wrong,
I don't try to un - der -
D
stand.
Let the

E7
devil take tomorrow.
A7
Lord, tonight I need a friend.
D.S. al Coda
CODA
Help me make it through the
D
G
D
night.

THE HIGHWAYMAN

Words and Music by
JIMMY WEBB

Moderately
Bm
mf
Bm
A
G
1. I was a high - way - man; a - long the coach roads I did
2.-4. (See additional lyrics)
Bm
A
G
D
ride, with sword and pis - tol by my
A
Em
Bm
A
side. Man - y a young maid lost her bau - bles to my

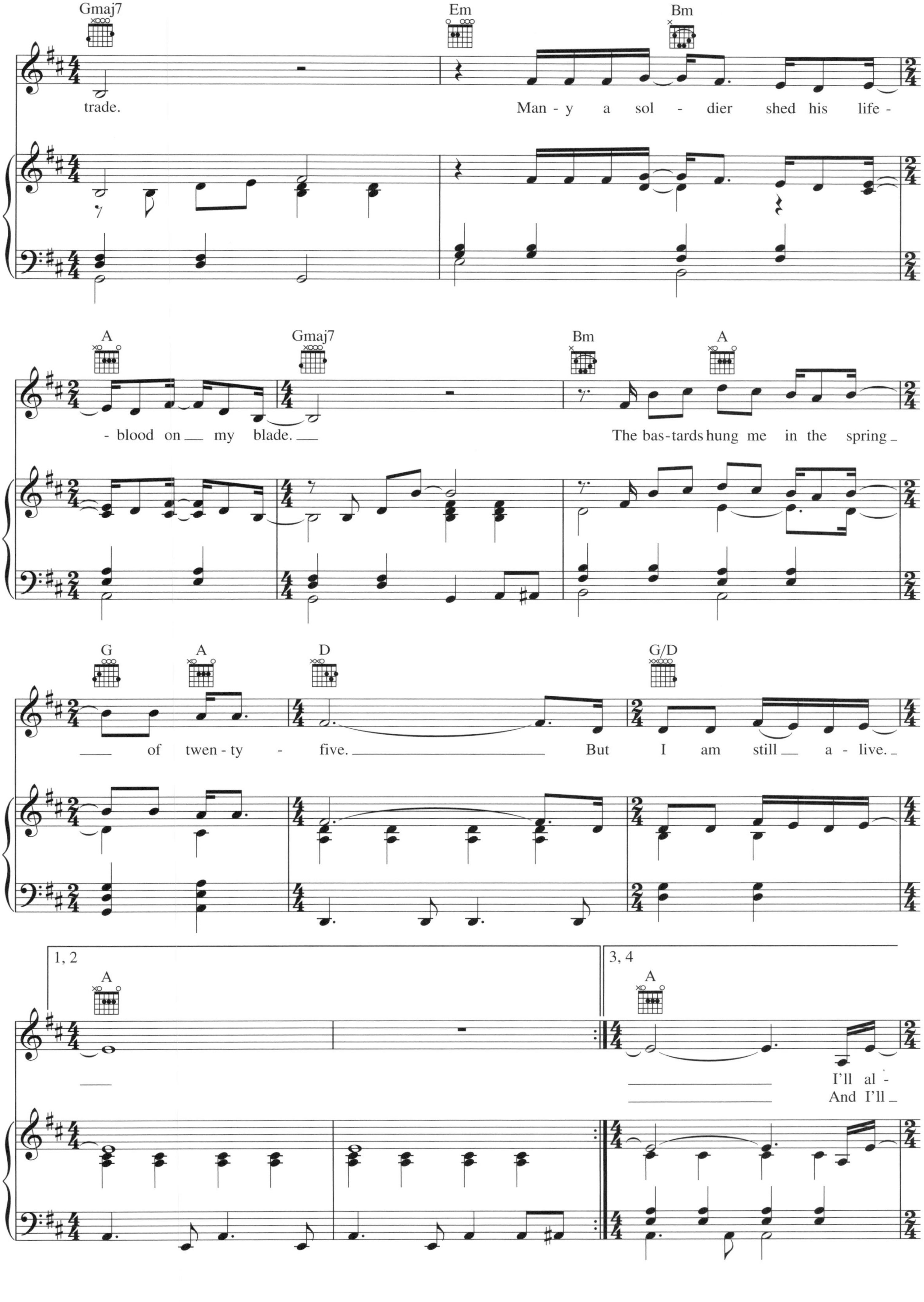
Gmaj7
Em
Bm
trade.
Man - y a sol - dier shed his life -
A
Gmaj7
Bm
A
- blood on my blade.
The bas-tards hung me in the spring
G
A
D
G/D
of twen - ty - five.
But I am still a - live.
1, 2
A
3, 4
A
I'll al -
And I'll

Additional Lyrics

2. I was a sailor,
   And I was born upon the tide,
   And with the sea I did abide.
   I sailed a schooner 'round the Horn to Mexico;
   I went aloft to furl the mainsail in a blow.
   And when the yards broke off, they say that I got killed.
   But I am living still.

3. I was a dam builder
   Across the river deep and wide,
   Where steel and water did collide.
   A place called Boulder on the wild Colorado,
   I slipped and fell into the wet concrete below.
   They buried me in that great tomb that knows no sound,
   But I am still around;
   I'll always be around, and around, and around,
   And around, and around, and around, and around.

4. I'll fly a starship
   Across the universe divide.
   And when I reach the other side,
   I'll find a place to rest my spirit if I can.
   Perhaps I may become a highwayman again,
   Or I may simply be a single drop of rain.
   But I remain.
   And I'll be back again, and again, and again,
   And again, and again, and again, and again.

I SWEAR

Words and Music by FRANK MYERS
and GARY BAKER

Moderately
mp
C
Am7
Em7
F/G
G
C
Am7
Em7
F/G
G
C
F/A
G/B
C
I see the ques - tions in ___ your eyes; ___ I know what's weigh -
I'll give you ev - 'ry - thing _ I can; ___ I'll build your dreams _

F G Am
- ing on your mind. But you can be sure
with these two hands. And we'll hang some mem -
F Gsus G
I know my part. 'Cause I'll
- 'ries on the wall. And when
3fr
C F/A G/B
stand be - side you through the years;
there's sil - ver in your hair,
C F G
you'll on - ly cry those hap - py tears.
won't have to ask if I still care.

Am
C/G
And though I'll make mis - takes,
'Cause as time turns the page, my
D/F♯
Gsus
3fr
G
C
I'll nev - er break your heart.
love won't age at all.
I swear by the moon
Am7
Em7
F
G
and the stars in the sky, I'll be there. I swear,
C
Am7
Em7
like a shad - ow that's by your side, I'll be there.

F G Dm7 Gsus G
For bet - ter or worse, till death do us part, I'll
Dm7
love you with ev - er - y beat
To Coda
1
Gsus G
of my heart, I swear.
C Am Em7 F/G G
2
Gsus G C Am7
of my heart, I swear.
Instrumental solo

Em7
Gsus
3fr
G
C
Am7
Em7
F/G
G
D.S. al Coda
Solo ends
I swear
CODA
Gsus
3fr
G
C
of my heart,
I swear.
Am
F
G
C
I swear.
rit.

HOLD ME

Words and Music by
K.T. OSLIN

Moderately
C
F/C
C
(Spoken:) Husband comes in, he says, "Wife, turn down the radio, turn off
(Spoken:) Husband says, "Wife, what do
mf
F
C
the T.V., listen to me. Let me tell you about my day." And she sits down and she listens, and he
you think?" Wife says, "It's very interesting. Before we talk about your day, let's talk about mine."
3
F/C
C
F/C
begins to speak: When I left here this morn-ing I was bound and de-ter-mined I was
And she says: When I left here this morn-ing I was bound and de-ter-mined I was

C
F/C
C
nev - er gon - na come back, nev - er, nev - er. I was
nev - er gon - na come back, nev - er, nev - er. I was
F
run - ning. I was run - ning from you, dar - ling. I was
run - ing. I was run - ning from you, dar - ling. I was
run - ning from my job. I was run - ning from the kid in me. He
run - ning from my job. I was run - ning from some wrink - les
nev - er knows when to stop. Got as far as the
no cream will stop. I got as far as the
C

Em/G Dm/G F G
edge of town, then I turned my car a-round and head-ed back
edge of town, then I turned my car a-round and I head-ed back to
1 C
2 C Dm/C C
to you.
you. Come here and hold me
Fmaj9 F6 C/G G7 C/G G7
tight - er. Tell me to-mor - row will be
Dm/C C Dm/C C
bright - er. Kiss me.

Fmaj9
F6
Kiss me a lit - tle hard - er.
G7
Dm/C
C
Don't kiss me like we're mar - ried. Kiss me like we're lov - ers.
F
F+
We looked at each oth - er and we start - ed to
F6
F+
G7
grin. This morn - ing it was o - ver,

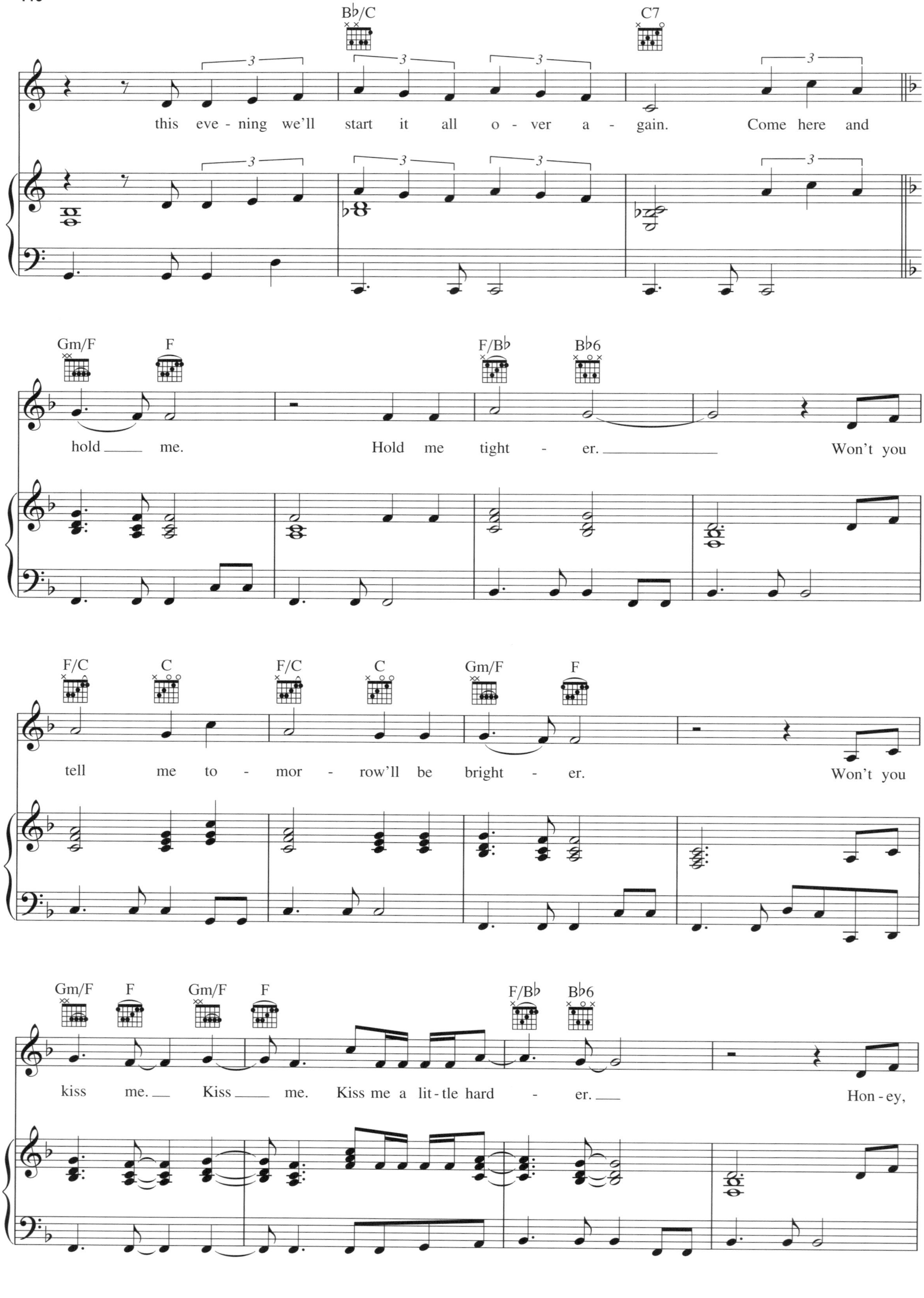
B♭/C
C7
this eve - ning we'll start it all o - ver a - gain. Come here and
Gm/F
F
F/B♭
B♭6
hold me. Hold me tight - er. Won't you
F/C
C
F/C
C
Gm/F
F
tell me to - mor - row'll be bright - er. Won't you
Gm/F
F
Gm/F
F
F/B♭
B♭6
kiss me. Kiss me. Kiss me a lit-tle hard - er. Hon-ey,

C7
Gm
3fr
F
3
don't kiss me like we're mar - ried, kiss me like we're lov - ers. And hold
B♭/C
F
B♭/C
me, hold
F
B♭/C
me, hold me.
F(add9)
Repeat and Fade

I HOPE YOU DANCE

Words and Music by TIA SILLERS
and MARK D. SANDERS

Moderately
Gm
3fr
E♭
3fr
B♭
F/A
mf
Gm
3fr
E♭
3fr
Fsus
F
1
2
I
B♭
hope you nev - er lose ___ your sense of won - der.
nev - er fear ___ those ___ moun - tains in the dis - tance.

Gm7
You get your fill to eat, but al - ways keep that
Nev - er set - tle for the path of least re -
hun - ger.
sist - ance.
Eb
May you nev - er take one
Liv - in' might mean tak - in'
sin - gle breath for grant - ed.
chanc - es, but they're worth tak - in'.
God for - bid
Lov - in' might
F
love ev - er leave you emp - ty - hand - ed.
be a mis - take, but it's worth mak - in'.

E♭ 3fr F
I hope you still feel small when you stand be-side the
Don't let some hell-bent heart leave you
B♭ E♭ 3fr F
o-cean. When-ev-er one door clos-es, I
bit-ter. When you come close to sell-in' out,
B♭
hope one more o-pens. Prom-ise me
re-con-sid-er. Give the heav-
Cm7 3fr B♭/D
that you'll give faith a fight-ing
ens a-bove more than just a pass-ing

E♭
3fr
chance.
glance.
And when you get the choice to
To Coda
Fsus
F
sit it out or dance,
I hope you dance.
1
Gm
3fr
E♭
3fr
B♭
F/A
Gm
3fr
E♭
3fr
I hope you dance.

Fsus F
2 Gm E♭
Time is a wheel in constant
I hope you
B♭ F/A Gm E♭
motion, always rolling us along.
I hope you dance.
Fsus F Gm E♭
Tell me, who wants to look back on their
I hope you dance.
3fr

B♭
F/A
Gm
E♭
3fr
youth and won - der where those years have gone?
I hope you dance.
Fsus
F
D.S. al Coda
(Verse 1)
I hope you still
CODA
dance...
N.C.
Dance,

Gm
E♭
3fr
Fsus
F
I hope you dance.
Gm
E♭
B♭
F/A
(Time is a wheel in con - stant mo - tion, al -
I hope you dance.
Gm
E♭
Fsus
F
- ways roll - ing us a - long.)
I hope you dance.

Gm
3fr
Eb
3fr
Bb
F/A
(Tell me, who wants to look back on their youth and won -
I hope _ you dance, ___
Gm
3fr
Eb
3fr
Repeat and Fade
Fsus
F
- der where ___ those years ___ have ___ gone?) ___
I hope _ you dance. ___
Optional Ending
Fsus
F
Bb
I hope ___ you dance. _
rit.

I STILL BELIEVE IN YOU

Words and Music by JOHN BARLOW JARVIS
and VINCE GILL

D/F♯
Bm
G(add9)
A7sus
A7
to prove and I'll make it up to you.
Chorus
D
C(add9)
Em7
D/F♯
I still be - lieve in you, with a love that will al - ways
G
A7
D
C(add9)
be. Stand - ing so strong and true, ba - by,
Em7
D/F♯
G
A7
1
D
I still be - lieve in you and me.

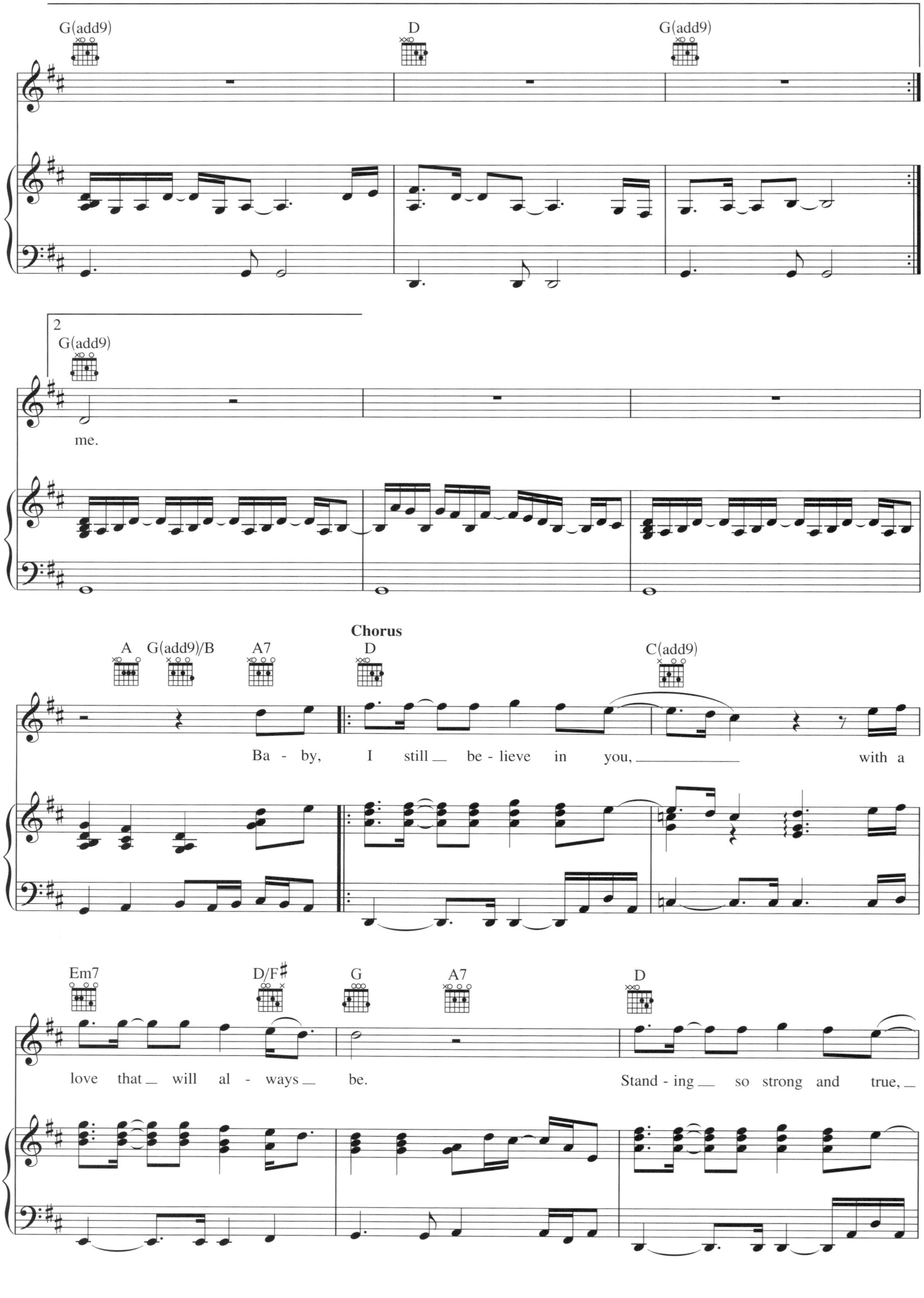
G(add9)
D
G(add9)
2
G(add9)
me.
Chorus
A
G(add9)/B
A7
D
C(add9)
Ba - by, I still __ be - lieve in you, __ with a
Em7
D/F♯
G
A7
D
love that __ will al - ways __ be.
Stand - ing __ so strong and true, __

Additional Lyrics

2. Somewhere along the way, I guess I just lost track,
   Only thinkin' of myself, never lookin' back.
   For all the times I've hurt you, I apologize,
   I'm sorry it took so long to finally realize.
   Give me the chance to prove
   That nothing's worth losing you.
   Chorus

IT'S FIVE O'CLOCK SOMEWHERE

Words and Music by JIM BROWN
and DON ROLLINS

Bm A D G
win - ter time, but it's Ju - ly. I'm get - tin' paid by the hou - r and
hell to pay, hey, but that's al - right. Ain't had a day off now in
D A D
old - er by the min - ute. My boss just pushed me o - ver the lim - it. I'd like to
o - ver a year. My Ja - mai - can va - ca - tion's gon - na start right here. If the
G D N.C. A N.C.
call him some - thin', I think I'll just call it a day.
phone's for me, you can tell 'em I've just sailed a - way.
D G A
Pour me some - thin' tall and strong,
(D.S.) pour me some - thin' tall and strong,
make it a hur - ri - cane be - fore I

D
G
go in - sane. It's on - ly half past twelve, but I don't care.
A
To Coda
1
N.C.
D
It's five o' - clock some - where.
G
A
D
2
D
Well, it's five o' - clock some - where.

G
A
D
G
A
D
Bm
G
I could pay off my tab, pour my - self in a cab and be
Em
A
D
Bm
back to work _ be - fore two. _ At a mo - ment like this, I

G Em A
can't help but won - der: What would Jim - my Buf - fet do?
D.S. al Coda
I'd say
CODA
N.C. D G
Pour me some-thin' tall and strong, make it a
A D
hur - ri - cane be - fore I go in - sane. It's on - ly half past twelve,
G A
but I don't care. And I don't care.

N.C.
D
It's five o'clock some - where.
G
A
D
Repeat and Fade
ad lib.
G
A
D
Optional Ending

JESUS TAKE THE WHEEL

Words and Music by BRETT JAMES,
HILLARY LINDSAY and GORDIE SAMPSON

1
Bm7
A
Gsus2
faith and gas - o - line. It'd been a long hard year. She had a
2
Bm7
A
Gsus2
she did - n't e - ven have time to cry. She was so scared. She threw her
D
N.C.
Dsus
D
hands up in the air: "Je - sus, take the wheel;
A
E
Bm
A/C♯
take it from my hands, 'cause I can't do this on my own.

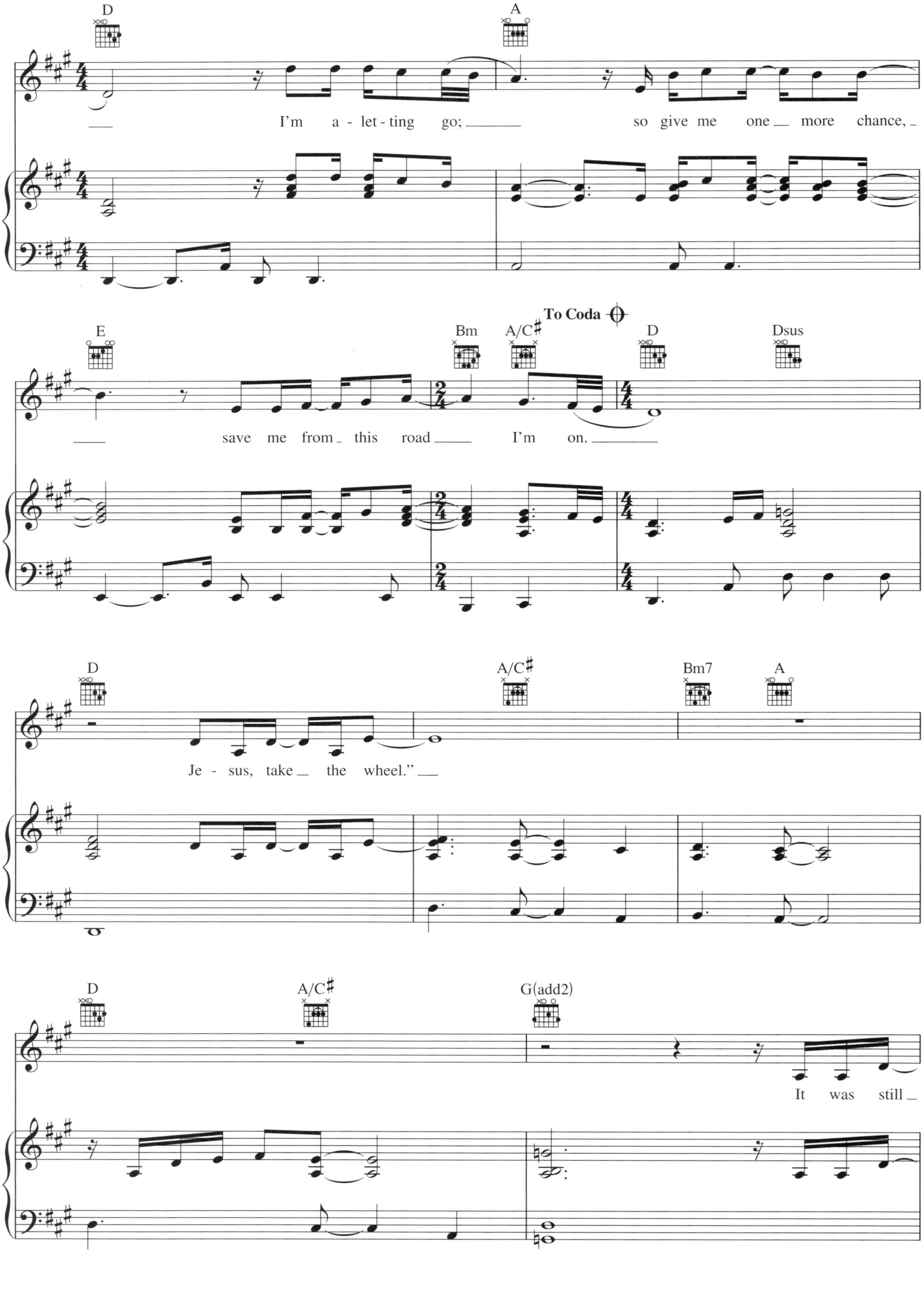
D
A
I'm a - let - ting go;
so give me one more chance,
E
Bm
A/C♯
To Coda
D
Dsus
save me from this road I'm on.
D
A/C♯
Bm7
A
Je - sus, take the wheel."
D
A/C♯
G(add2)
It was still

D A/C♯ Bm7 A
getting colder when she made it to the shoulder and the car came to a stop; and she cried
D A/C♯ Bm7 A
when she saw that baby in the back seat, sleeping like a rock. And for the first
D A/C♯ Bm7 A
time in a long time, she bowed her head to pray. She said, "I'm
Gsus2 D/F♯ Gsus2
sorry for the way I've been living my life; I know I've got to change. So from
3

D
Dsus
D
D.S. al Coda
now on, to - night,
Je - sus, take the wheel;
CODA
D
Dsus
D
Oh, Je - sus take the wheel."
A
E
Bm7
A/C♯
D
A
"Oh, I'm a - let - ting go;
so give me one more

E
Bm
A/C♯
chance, save me from this road I'm on,
D
Bm
A/C♯
D
Dsus
from this road I'm on.
D
D
A/C♯
Bm7
A
Je - sus, take the wheel.
Oh, take it,
1
D
A/C♯
Bm7
A
take it from me."
Vocal continues ad lib.
2
D
A/C♯
G(add2)

KING OF THE ROAD

Words and Music by
ROGER MILLER

Moderately, with a bounce
N.C.
p
C
F
G
C
mp
(1., D.S.) Trail - er for sale or rent, rooms to let, fif - ty cents.
(2.) Third box - car mid - night train, des - ti - na - tion: Ban - gor, Maine.
F
G
N.C.
Dm
No phone, no pool, no pets; I ain't got no cig - a - rettes. Ah, but
Old worn - out suit and shoes; I don't pay no un - ion dues. I smoke
C
F
G
C
two hours of push - ing broom buys a eight by twelve four bit room.
old sto - gies I have found, short but not too big a - round.
I'm a

F
G
To Coda
1
C
N.C.
man of means by no means, king of the road.
2
C
G
C
F
G7
I know ev-er-y en-gi-neer on ev-er-y train, all of the chil-dren and
C
F
all of their names, and ev-er-y hand-out in ev-er-y town, and
G7
N.C.
D.S. al Coda
ev-'ry lock that ain't locked when no one's a-round. I sing:
CODA
C
3

KISS AN ANGEL GOOD MORNIN'

Words and Music by
BEN PETERS

G
I've al-ways got a smil-in' face,
The se-cret I'm speak-in' of
G7
C
an-y-time and an-y place, and
is a wom-an and a man in love, and the
D
G
ev-'ry time they ask me why, I just smile and say:
an-swer is in this song that I al-ways sing:
D7
You've got to kiss an an-gel good morn-in' and

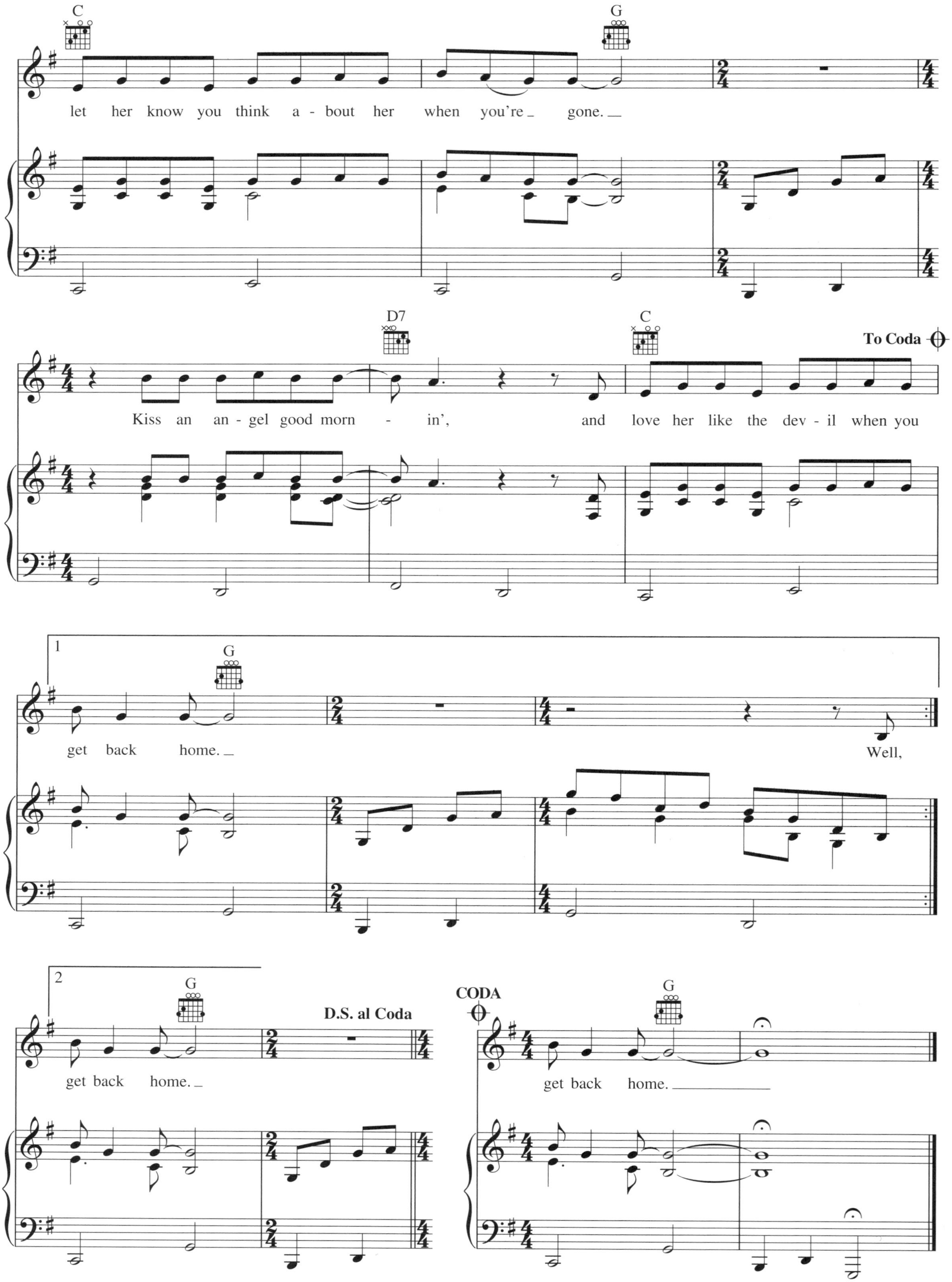
C
G
let her know you think a - bout her when you're _ gone. _
D7
C
To Coda
Kiss an an - gel good morn - in', and love her like the dev - il when you
1
G
get back home. _
Well,
2
G
D.S. al Coda
get back home. _
CODA
G
get back home. _

LITTLE GREEN APPLES

Words and Music by
BOBBY RUSSELL

C6
Cm6
3fr
squeez-es it says, "How you feel-in', Hon?" And I
Am7
D7
Am7
D7
G6
look a-cross at smil-ing lips that warm my heart and see the morn-ing sun.
Am7
D7
Am7
D7
And if that's not lov-in' me, then all I've
Am7
D7
Am7
D7
G
got to say, God did-n't make lit-tle green ap-ples, and

Gmaj7
Am7
D7
Am7
D7
it don't rain in In - dia - nap'-lis in the sum-mer - time. _ There's
Am7
D7
Am7
D7
G6
To Coda
no such thing as Doc - tor Seuss, Dis - ney - land and Moth - er Goose is no nurs - 'ry rhyme.
G
Gmaj7
Am7
God did - n't make lit - tle green ap - ples, and it don't rain in In - dia - nap'-lis in the sum-mer - time. _
D7
Am7
D7
Am7
D7
And when my - self is feel - in' low I think a - bout her face a - glow to

G6
Am7
D9
ease my mind.
Some-
Am7
D9
Am7
D7
D9
G6
times I call her up at home knowing she's bus - y.
Am7
D7
Am7
D7
And ask if she could get a-way and meet me and grab a
G6
G7
bite to eat.
And she drops what she's do - in' and

C6
Cm6
3fr
hur-ries down to meet me and I'm al - ways late. But
Am7
D7
Am7
D7
G6
D.S. al Coda
she sits wait-ing pa - tient - ly and smiles when she first sees me 'cause she's made that way.
CODA
G
Gmaj7
God did - n't make lit - tle green ap - ples and it don't rain in In - dia - nap' - lis in the
Am7
D7
Repeat and Fade
Optional Ending
G
sum - mer - time.

LIVE LIKE YOU WERE DYING

Words and Music by CRAIG WISEMAN
and TIM J. NICHOLS

G
C
my ear - ly for - ties with a lot of life be - fore me when a
Em
D
Csus2
3fr
mo - ment came that stopped me on a dime.
I spent
G
C
most of the next days look - in' at the x - rays
Em
D
D(add4)
3fr
Cmaj7
and talk - in' 'bout the op - tions and talk - in' 'bout sweet time."

Em
G+/D♯
I asked him, when it sank in, if this might real-ly be the real end, how's it
G/D
Cmaj9
hit you when you get that kind of news?
Man, what'd you do?
N.C.
G
And he said, "I went sky - div - in', I went
C
Em
D
Rock-y Moun-tain climb - in', I went two-point - sev - en sec - onds on a bull

C
G
named Fu Man - chu. And I loved deep - er and I
B7
Em
D
spoke sweet - er and I gave for-give - ness I'd been de-ny -
C
To Coda
- in'." And he said, "Some - day I hope you get the chance
D
G
to live like you were dy - in'."

Csus2
3fr
Em7
Csus2
3fr
G
He said, "I was fi - nal - ly the hus - band
C
Em
D
that most the time I was - n't and I be - came a friend a friend would like to have.
C
G
And all the sud - den go - in' fish - in' was - n't

C
Em
D
such an im - po - si - tion and I went three times that year I lost my
C
Em
dad. Well, I, I fin-'lly read the Good Book and I
G+/D#
G/D
took a good long hard look at what I'd do if I could do it all a - gain.
C
D/C
Csus2
3fr
Cmaj7
Cmaj9
N.C.
D.S. al Coda
And then I went

CODA
D
Em
to live like you were dy - in', like to-mor-
G+/D#
G/D
- row was a gift and you got e - ter - ni - ty to think
C
a - bout what you'd do with it,
what could you do
D/C
C
with it,
what did I do with it,
what would I do

C(add9)
N.C.
A
with it?
Sky - div - in', I went
D
F♯m7
Rock - y Moun - tain climb - in', I went two - point - sev - en sec -
E
D
- onds on a bull named Fu Man - chu. And I
A
C♯7
loved deep - er and I spoke sweet -

F♯m
A/E
D
-er and I watched an ea - gle as it was fly -
E/D
D
- in'." And he said, "Some - day I hope
E
A
you get the chance to live like you were dy - in',
D(add9)
A
to live like you were dy - in',

D(add9)
A
to live like you were dy - in',
D(add9)
A
to live like you were dy - in',
D(add9)
A
to live like you were dy -
D(add9)
A

D(add9)
A
in'."
D(add9)
A
D(add9)
Repeat and Fade
A
D(add9)
Optional Ending
A

MEAN

Words and Music by
TAYLOR SWIFT

Moderately fast

B
Asus2
voice like nails on a chalk - board call - ing me out when I'm wound - ed.
C♯m
B
A
You, pick - ing on the weak - er man.
B5
Well, you can take me down
E
A
B
with just one sin - gle blow.

Asus2
But you don't know what you don't know.
E B C#m
Some - day I'll be liv - ing in a big ole
A E B
cit - y, and all you're ev - er gon - na be is
A E
mean. Some - day
4fr

B C♯m A
I'll be big e - nough so you can't hit me, and
E B A
all you're ev - er gon - na be is mean.
N.C. E
Why you got - ta be so mean?
D E To Coda B/D♯ C♯m
You, with your

B
A
switch - ing sides and your wild - fire lies and your hu - mil - i - a - tion.
C♯m
4fr
B
A
You have point - ed out my flaws a - gain, as if I
N.C.
C♯m
4fr
B
don't al - read - y see them. I walk with my head down, try'n' to
A
C♯m
4fr
block you out 'cause I'll nev - er im - press you. I just

B
A
wan - na feel o - kay a - gain.
B
E
I bet you got pushed a - round. Some - bod - y
A
B
made you cold. But the cy - cle ends right now 'cause you
A
can't lead me down that road, and you don't know what you

N.C.
D.S. al Coda
CODA
B
A
don't know.
B
A
And I can
B
E
see you years from now in a bar,
talk-ing o-ver a
A
B
foot-ball game
with that same big, loud o-pin-ion, but

E
A
B
no - bod - y's lis - ten - ing. Washed up and rant -
C♯m
4fr
B
- ing a - bout the same old bit - ter
A
B
things, drunk and grum - bling on
C♯m
4fr
B
A
a - bout how I can't sing.

N.C.
E
B
But all you are is mean.
C♯m
A
E
All you are is mean, and a
B
C♯m
A
li - ar, and pa - thet - ic, and a - lone in life, and
E
B
C♯m
mean and mean and mean and

A
E
B
mean. But some - day I'll be
Some - day
C♯m
4fr
A
E
liv - ing in a big ole cit - y, and all you're
B
A
ev - er gon - na be is mean. Oh,
E
B
C♯m
4fr
some - day I'll be big e - nough so you can't

1
A
E
B
hit me, and all you're ev - er gon - na be is
A
mean. Why you got - ta be so...
2
E
B
all you're ev - er gon - na be is
A
E
mean. Why you got - ta be so mean?

LOVE CAN BUILD A BRIDGE

Words and Music by PAUL OVERSTREET,
JOHN JARVIS and NAOMI JUDD

Am7(add4)
3fr
Fsus2
C/G
sea of bro - ken dreams. When all your hopes are sink - ing,
that you might see. The first step is to re - al - ize that it
G7sus
G7
C
F
let me show you what love means.
all be - gins with you and me.
Love can build a
G7
Dm
G7/B
bridge be - tween your heart and
C
F
G
C
C/E
mine. Love can build a

F
To Coda
1
C/G
G7
bridge, don't you think it's time?
Don't you think it's time?
C(add9)
D7sus/C
C(add9)
D7sus/C
2
C/G
G7
I would
Don't you think it's time?
C
F
G7
Dm
G7/B

C F G C C/E F
C/G G7 C Am
When we stand to-geth - er,
G7/B C Dm7 C/E
it's our fin - est hour. We can do any-y-thing, an-y-thing, if we
F G D.S. al Coda
keep be-liev - in' in the pow - er.
CODA
C/G G7
Don't you think it's time?

C F G C F G7
Love can build a bridge be -
Dm G7/B C F G C C/E
tween your heart and mine. Love can build a
F C/G G7
bridge, don't you think it's time? Don't you think it's time?
C(add9) D7sus/C C(add9)

D7sus/C
C(add9)
Don't you think it's time?
F
C(add9)
F
Love and on - ly love;
C(add9)
F
love and on - ly love.
C(add9)
F
C(add9)
rit.

MY WOMAN MY WOMAN MY WIFE

Words and Music by
MARTY ROBBINS

F
G7
C
too many-y hours in the sun.
smiles when I want to stop.
Eyes that show some dis-ap-
Lips that are wea - ry, but
Em
F
G7
point - ment, and there's been quite a lot in her life.
ten - der with love that strength - ens my life.
But
A
C
C+
F
C
G7
she's the foun-da - tion I lean on,
saint in a dress made of ging - ham,
my wom - an, my wom - an, my
C
F
Em
wife.
Two lit-tle ba-bies were born in the spring, but

F
C
Am
died when the win - ter was new.
I lost con - trol of my
Em
D7
G7
mind and my soul, but my wom-an's faith car-ried us through.
C
Em
F
When she reach - es that riv - er,
Lord, you know what she's
G7
C
Em
worth,
give her that man-sion up yon - der,
'cause she's

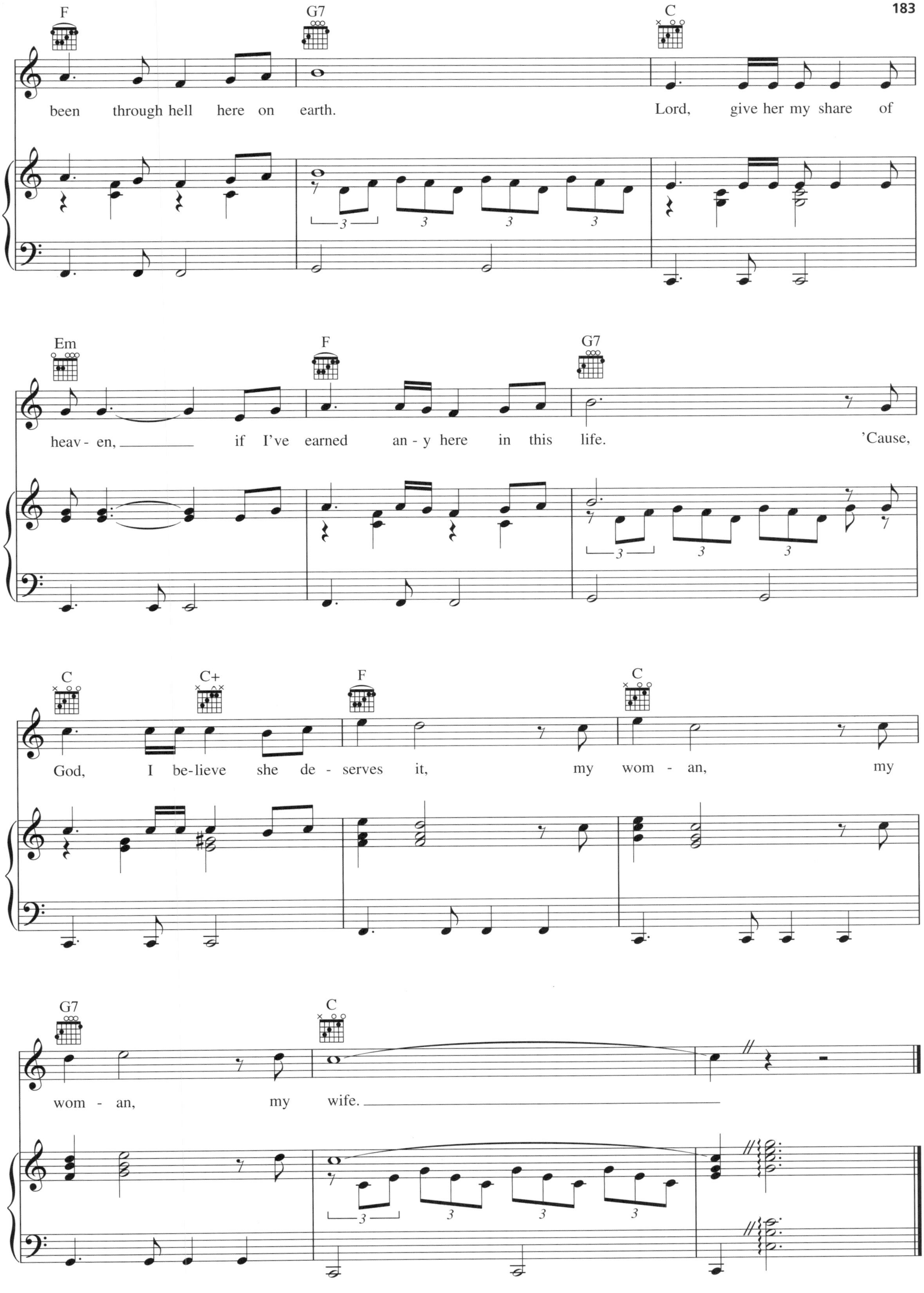
F G7 C
been through hell here on earth. Lord, give her my share of
Em F G7
heav - en, if I've earned an - y here in this life. 'Cause,
C C+ F C
God, I be-lieve she de - serves it, my wom - an, my
G7 C
wom - an, my wife.

NEED YOU NOW

Words and Music by HILLARY SCOTT,
CHARLES KELLEY, DAVE HAYWOOD
and JOSH KEAR

A
C♯m
- der if I ev - er crossed your mind.
A
For me it hap - pens all the time. It's a
𝄋
E
quar - ter af - ter one,
(1.,D.S.) I'm all a - lone
(2.) I'm a lit - tle drunk
and I need
G♯m
you now.
Said

E
I would - n't call, (1.,2.) but I lost all con - trol and I need
(D.S.) but I'm a lit - tle drunk
G♯m
4fr
you now. And I don't
A
know how I can do with - out. I
To Coda
1
just need you now.

C♯m
An -
2
C♯m
B
E
A
B
C♯m
B
E
3
A
B
A
Guess I'd rath - er hurt than feel

C♯m
B
D.S. al Coda
noth - in' at all. It's a
CODA
E
G♯m
E
I just need you now.
G♯m

E
G♯m
4fr
Oh, ba -
- by, I need you now.
E
G♯m
4fr
E
Emaj7

NINE TO FIVE

from NINE TO FIVE

Words and Music by
DOLLY PARTON

C
G
out on the street, the traf - fic starts jump - ing, with folks like me on the
wait - in' for the day your ship - 'll come in, and the tide's gon - na turn and
D
G
To Coda
C
job from nine to five.
it's all gon - na roll your way.
Work - ing nine to five,
Nine to five,
what a way to make a liv - ing; bare - ly
for ser - vice and de - vo - tion; you would
G
get - ting by, it's all tak - ing and no giv - ing. They just
think that I would de - serve a fair pro - mo - tion. Want to

C
use your mind, and they nev - er give you
move a - head, but the boss won't seem to
A7
cred - it; it's e - nough to drive you
let me. I swear some - times that man is
1
D7
cra - zy, if you let it.
2
D7
out to get me.
G
mp
N.C.
D.S. al Coda

CODA
C
nine to five, what a way to make a liv - ing; bare - ly
Nine to five, they've got you where they want you; there's a
G
get - ting by, it's all tak - ing and no giv - ing. They just
bet - ter life, and you dream a - bout it, don't you? It's a
C
use your mind, and you nev - er get the cred - it; it's e -
rich man's game, no mat - ter what they call it; and you
A7
D7
Repeat and Fade
nough to drive you cra - zy, if you let it.
spend your life put - ting mon - ey in his pock - et.

ON THE ROAD AGAIN

Words and Music by
WILLIE NELSON

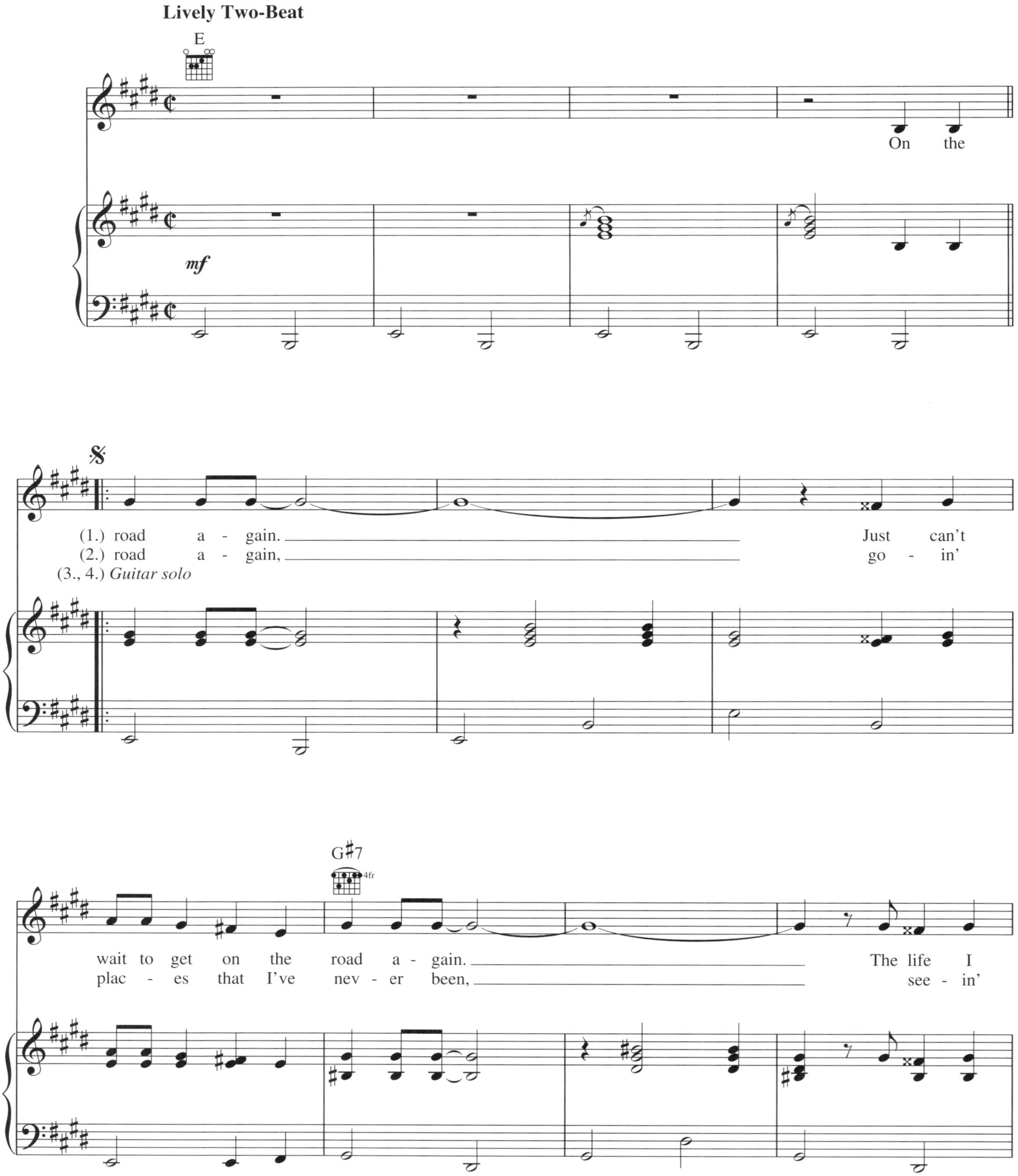
Lively Two-Beat
E
mf
On the
(1.) road a - gain. Just can't
(2.) road a - gain, go - in'
(3., 4.) Guitar solo
G#7
4fr
wait to get on the road a - gain. The life I
plac - es that I've nev - er been, see - in'

F♯m
A
love is mak - ing mu - sic with my friends, and I can't wait to get
things that I may nev - er see a - gain, and I can't wait to get
B7
1, 3
E
2, 4
E
on the road a - gain. On the
on the road a - gain.
E7
A
Solo ends
On the road a - gain. Like a band of gyp - sies,
E
we go down the high - way. We're the

A
best of friends, in - sist - ing that the world keep turn - ing
E
B7
our way, and our way is on the
E
road a - gain. Just can't wait to get on the
G♯7
4fr
road a - gain. The life I love is mak - in'

F♯m
A
B7
To Coda
mu - sic with my friends, and I can't wait to get on the road a -
E
D.S. al Coda
(take repeat)
gain.
CODA
E
gain. And
A
B7
E
E7
I can't wait to get on the road a - gain.
A
B
B7
E
A
E

PASSIONATE KISSES

Words and Music by
LUCINDA WILLIAMS

Moderately
D
A/C♯
legato
mp
With pedal
Bm
G
Bright Rock
D
A
Bm
G
mf
D
A
Bm
Is __ it too much to ask? __ I want a com-fort-a-ble bed __ that won't
Is __ it too much to de-mand? _ I want a full house _ and a

G
D
A
hurt my back, food to fill me up, and
rock 'n' roll band, pens that won't run out of ink, and
Bm
G
D
warm clothes, and all that stuff.
cool qui - et and time to think.
Should - n't I have
F♯m7
Bm
G
this, should - n't I have this, should - n't I have all of this and
D
G
D
pas - sion - ate kiss - es, pas - sion - ate

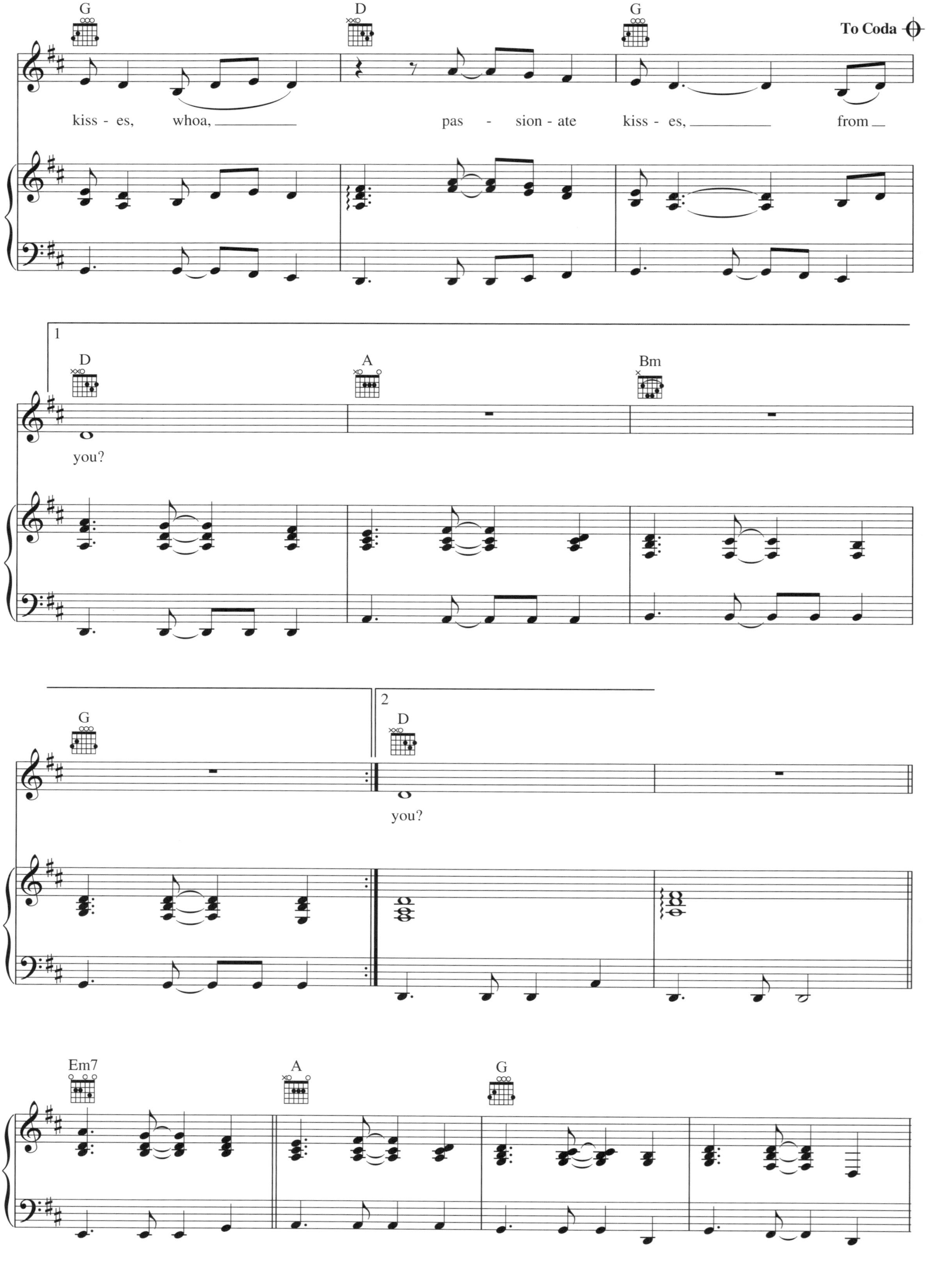
G
D
G
To Coda
kiss - es, whoa, pas - sion - ate kiss - es, from
1
D
A
Bm
you?
G
2
D
you?
Em7
A
G

Em7
F♯7
Bm
Asus
A
D
A
Do I want too much? Am I go-
Bm
G
D
-ing o-ver-board to want that touch?
I shout it out
A
Bm
G
D.S. al Coda
to the night. Give me what I de-serve, 'cause it's my right.

CODA
D
G
D
you?
Pas - sion - ate
G
D
G
kiss - es, pas - sion - ate kiss - es, whoa,
D
G
D
pas - sion - ate kiss - es, from you.
(Sing 1st time only)
A
Bm
G
Repeat and Fade

WHITE HORSE

Words and Music by TAYLOR SWIFT
and LIZ ROSE

C5
3fr
Fsus2
Am7
as I paced back and forth all this time 'cause I hon - est - ly be-lieved in
Fsus2
Am7
Fsus2
you. Hold - ing on, the days drag on. Stu-pid girl,
Gsus
3fr
G
I should-'ve known, I should-'ve known that I'm not a prin -
C
Am7
Fsus2
- cess, this ain't a fair - y tale. I'm not the one you'll sweep off her feet, lead

Gsus
3fr
C
her up the stair - well. This ain't Hol - ly - wood, this is a small
Am7
Fsus2
G
town. I was a dream - er be - fore you went and let me down. Now it's too
Am7
G/B
F
To Coda
late for you and your white horse to come a - round.
C5
3fr
May-be I was na - ive,

Fsus2
Am7
Fsus2
got lost in your eyes and nev - er real - ly had a chance.
C
F
My mis - take, I did - n't know to be in love you had to
Am7
Fsus2
Am7
fight to have the up - per hand. I had so man - y dreams a - bout you
Fsus2
Gsus
3fr
G
D.S. al Coda
and me; hap - py end - ings. Now I know that I'm not a prin-

CODA
C
Am
F
Gsus
3fr
Am7
G/B
And there you are on your
F
C
G/B
F
knees,
beg - gin' for for - give - ness,
beg - gin' for me,
C
G/B
F
B♭
just like I al - ways want - ed.
But I'm so sor - ry.

C
Am7
'Cause I'm not your prin - cess, this ain't a fair - y tale. I'm gon - na find
Fsus2
G
some - one some - day who might ac - tu - 'ly treat me well. This is a
C
Am7
Fsus2
big world, that was a small town there in my rear - view mir - ror dis - ap - pear -
G
Am
G/B
F
in' now. And it's too late for you and your white horse, now it's too

Am
G/B
F
late for you and your white horse to catch me
C5
3fr
Fsus2
Am7
now.
Oh,
Fsus2
Csus2
3fr
F
try and catch me now,
oh.
Am
F
C
It's too late to catch me now.
rit.

STAY

Words and Music by
JENNIFER NETTLES

Slowly
E5
B
I've been sit-ting here star-ing at the clock on the wall;
mp
With pedal

E5
B
and I've been lay-ing here pray-ing, pray-ing she won't call.
It's just an-

F♯m7
A5
5fr
oth-er call from home; and you'll get it and be gone, and I'll be cry-

E5
B
E5
- ing.
And I'll be beg-ging you, ba-by,
You keep tell-ing me, ba-by,
B
E5
beg you not to leave;
but I'll be left here wait - ing with my
there will come a time
when you will leave her arms and for-
B
F♯m7
heart on my sleeve, oh, for the next time we'll be here. Seems
ev - er be in mine. But, I don't think that's the truth; and I
A5
5fr
E5
like a mil - lion years, and I think I'm dy - ing.
don't like be - ing used, and I'm tired of wait - ing.

B
F♯m7
What do I have to do to make
It's too much pain to have
A5
you see
to bear,
F♯m7
A5
she can't love you like me?
to love a man you have to share.
B
Why don't you stay?
𝄋
Esus2
1.,2. I'm down on my knees.
3. I'm up off my knees.
Asus2
C♯m7/G♯
F♯m7
I'm so tired of be - ing lone - ly.
I'm so tired of be - ing lone - ly.
Don't I give you what you need?
You can't give me what I need.
5fr
4fr

B
B♯dim
3fr
C♯m
4fr
B
When she calls you to go,
When she begs you not to go,
there is one thing you should know:
there is one thing you should know:
Asus2
C♯m7/G♯
4fr
F♯m7
we don't have to live this way.
I don't have to live this way.
Asus2
B
To Coda
1
E5
B
Ba-by, why don't you stay?
Yeah.
F♯m7
A5
5fr
B
2
E5
3
I can't
3

F♯m7
A
take it an - y long - er, but my will is get - ting strong - er, and I
Esus2
B
think I know just what I have to do. I can't
F♯m7
E/G♯
A
waste an - oth - er min - ute af - ter all that I've put in it. I've
E5
B
giv - en you my best; why does she get the best of you? So

F♯m7
A5
5fr
next time you find you wan - na leave her bed for
B
E/B
B
D.S. al Coda
mine, why don't you stay?
CODA
E5
B
Yeah. Oh,
F♯m7
A5
5fr
B
E5
oh, whoa.
rit.

STRANGER IN MY HOUSE

Words and Music by
MIKE REID

Moderately
Dm
C
G
G9
9fr
mf
With pedal

Dm
C
G

Dm

C
G
G9
9fr
1
G

2
G
Dm
C
There's a si - lence here __ be - tween __ us
star - ing out __ the win - dow,
G
Dm
I've nev - er heard be - fore. ____ And I can't find __ the love __
a bil - lion miles a - way. ____ And when I ask if she's al - right, __
C
G
____ in her eyes ____ an - y - more. ____ There's some
____ she nev - er has too much to say. ____ Is it
Gm9
3fr
Dm7
chang - es go - ing on ____ I'm be - gin - ning to un - der - stand. __
some - bod - y we both know, ____ or some - bod - y she just met? __

Gm9
3fr
When I'm hold - ing her, I swear I feel the
Is she lov - ing him in her mind while she's
A5
5fr
N.C.
Dm
pres-ence of an - oth - er man.
ly - ing here in my bed?
There's a stran - ger in my house,
Gm
3fr
Am7
A5
5fr
some-bod - y here that I can't see. A
Dm
Gm
3fr
Am7
stran - ger in my house,
some-bod - y here try - ing to

1 A5
Dm
C
G
take her a-way from_ me._
G
2
A5
She's just take her a-way from_ me._
Dm
C
G
G9
Dm
C
G

Dm
C
G
G9
9fr
Instrumental solo
1
2
G
G
B♭maj7
Solo ends
Sus - pi - cions lead to ques -
Dm
- tions, and ques - tions to al - i - bis.
Is it
B♭maj7
Asus
just my im - ag - i - na - tion,
or has her love turned in - to lies?

A5
5fr
N.C.
Dm
Gm
3fr
There's a stran - ger in my house,
Am7
A5
5fr
Dm
some-bod - y here that I can't see. A stran - ger in my house,
Gm
3fr
Repeat and Fade
Am7
A5
5fr
some-bod - y here try'n' to take her a - way. A
Optional Ending
Am7
A5
5fr
Dm
some-bod - y here try - ing to take her a - way from me.

A VERY SPECIAL LOVE SONG

Words and Music by
BILLY SHERRILL and NORRIS WILSON

F/G
G7
1
C
C+
2
C
love song, oh.
E♭
3fr
F
So don't be sur-prised if you're sit-tin' a-lone and you hear
B♭
E♭
3fr
F
it, 'cause I'm gon-na sing it to the whole big lone-ly
B♭
D7
3
world.
So turn your ra-di-o way down low and get

Gm
Cm/E♭
G+
G
3fr
near it, and I'll tell the world I love you, girl.
F/G
G7
C
C+
Babe, if there's an ounce of love I'm gon-na give it to you,
C
Dm7
babe. If there's a breath of life I'm gon-na live it
F
G7
Em
Am
ev-'ry way for you, and oh, the whole night through

D9 D7 Fmaj7/G G7 F/G G7 F/G G7
4fr
sing - in' just for you a ver - y spe - cial love song. Hmm
C C+ C
for you.
Adim F G Em Am
D7 Fmaj7/G G7 F/G G G9 G7 C
9fr

WHERE WERE YOU
(When the World Stopped Turning)

Words and Music by
ALAN JACKSON

Moderately fast
C
mf
C
G
Where were you when the world stopped turn - in' that Sep - tem - ber
C
day?
Out in the yard with your wife and chil - dren or
Teach - in' a class full of in - no - cent chil - dren or

G C F
work-in' on some stage in L. A.? Did you stand there in shock at the
driv-in' on some cold in-ter-state? Did you feel guilt-y 'cause
3
C F C
sight of that black smoke ris-in' a-gainst that blue sky? Did you
you're a sur-viv-or, in a crowd-ed room did you feel a-lone? Did you
F C Am
shout out in an-ger in fear for your neigh-bor, or did you just sit down and
call up your moth-er and tell her you love her? Did you dust off that Bi-ble at
F G C
cry? Did you weep for the chil-dren, they
home? Did you o-pen your eyes and hope

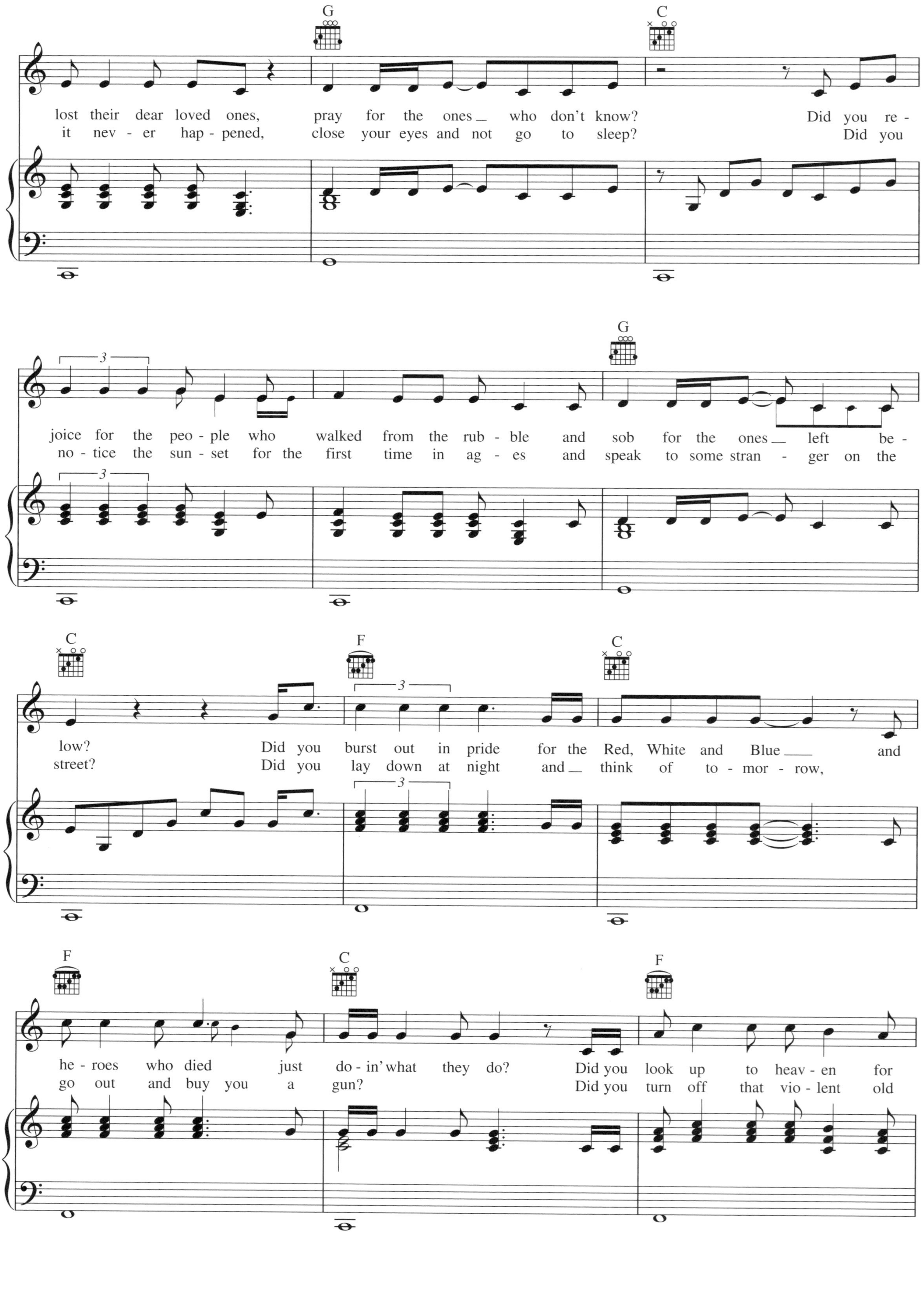
G
C
lost their dear loved ones, pray for the ones who don't know? Did you re-
it nev - er hap - pened, close your eyes and not go to sleep? Did you
G
joice for the peo - ple who walked from the rub - ble and sob for the ones left be -
no - tice the sun - set for the first time in ag - es and speak to some stran - ger on the
C
F
C
low? Did you burst out in pride for the Red, White and Blue and
street? Did you lay down at night and think of to - mor - row,
F
C
F
he - roes who died just do - in' what they do? Did you look up to heav - en for
go out and buy you a gun? Did you turn off that vio - lent old

C
To Coda
Am
F
some kind of an-swer and look at your-self and what real-ly mat-ters?
mov-ie you're watch-in' and
C
I'm just a sing-er of sim-ple songs. I'm not a
F
C
F
real po-lit-i-cal man. I watch C-N-N, but I'm not
C
Am
F
sure I can tell you the dif-f'rence in I-raq and I-ran. But

C
F
I know Je - sus and I talk to God and I re - mem - ber this from when I was
C
F
C
young: faith, hope and love are some good things He gave us
G
F
G/F
F
G
D.S. al Coda
and the great - est is love.
CODA
Am
F
G/F
F
turn on "I Love Lu - cy" re - runs? Did you go to a church and hold

C
F
C
hands with some stran - ger, stand in line to give your own blood? Did you
F
C
Am
just stay home and cling tight to your fam-'ly, thank God you have some-bod - y to love?
F
F
I'm just a sing - er of
C
F
C
sim - ple songs. I'm not a real po - lit - i - cal man. I watch

F C Am
C - N - N, but I'm not sure I can tell you the dif - f'rence in I - raq and I -
3
F C
ran. But I know Je - sus and I talk to God and I re -
F C F
mem - ber this from when I was young: faith, hope and love are some
3
C G F G
1
good things He gave us and the great - est is love.

2
F G/F F G F G/F
love, and the great - est is love,
F G F G/F F
and the great - est is love.
C
Where were you when the world stopped turn - in'
rit.
G N.C. C
that Sep - tem - ber day?

WHERE'VE YOU BEEN

Words and Music by
DON HENRY and JON VEZNER

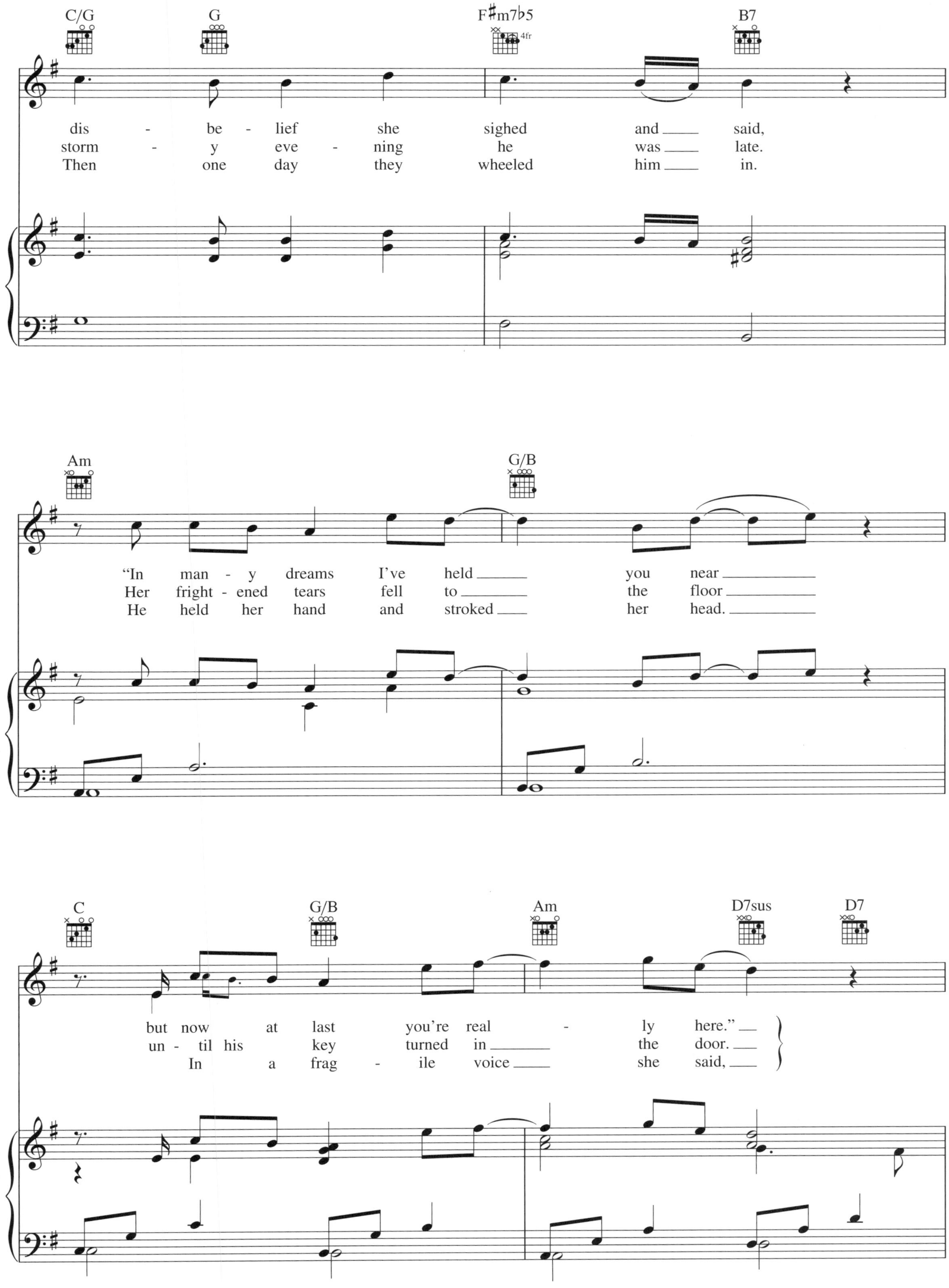
C/G G F♯m7♭5 B7
dis - be - lief she sighed and said,
storm - y eve - ning he was late.
Then one day they wheeled him in.
Am G/B
"In man - y dreams I've held you near
Her fright - ened tears fell to the floor
He held her hand and stroked her head.
C G/B Am D7sus D7
but now at last you're real - ly here."
un - til his key turned in the door.
In a frag - ile voice she said,

G
Em7
C
Cmaj7
Where have you been?
I've looked for you for-ev-er and a
G
To Coda
Em
C
day.
Where have you been?
Em
D7/F♯
1
G
2
G
I'm just not my-self when you're a - way.
way.
C
D/F♯
G
Cmaj7
They'd nev-er spent a night a-part.
For

Em7
C
six - ty years she heard him snore.
Now they're in the hos -
G/B
Am
D7
G/D
D7
D.S. al Coda
- pi - tal in sep-'rate beds on dif-f'rent floors.
rit.
CODA
G
Em
C
Where have you been?
I'm just not my-self when you're a -
Em7
G/D
D7
C(add9)
way.
No, I'm just not my-self when you're a - way.
rit.

YOU DECORATED MY LIFE

Words and Music by DEBBIE HUPP
and BOB MORRISON

C/G
bal - ance was right. Then you
you came a - long. And you
G
add - ed some mu - sic; ev - 'ry
brought out the col - ors; what a
C/G
Gmaj9
note was in place, and an - y - bod - y could see all the
gen - tle sur - prise. Now I'm a - ble to see all the
C/G
chang - es in me by the look on my face.
things life can be shin - ing soft in your eyes.

D C D G Gmaj9 C
And you dec - o - rat - ed my
mf
G Gmaj9 C Bm7 Em
life; cre - at - ed a world
Em/D Am7 D7
where dreams are a part. And
G Gmaj9 C G Gmaj9
you dec - o - rat - ed my life

C Bm7 Em Em/D
by paint-ing your love all o-ver my heart.
Am7 D7 G
You dec-o-rat-ed my life.
B/F# B
1
D/C C D/C C
Like a
decresc.
mp
2
D/C C D/C C Gmaj7

YOU'RE STILL THE ONE

Words and Music by SHANIA TWAIN
and R.J. LANGE

Slowly

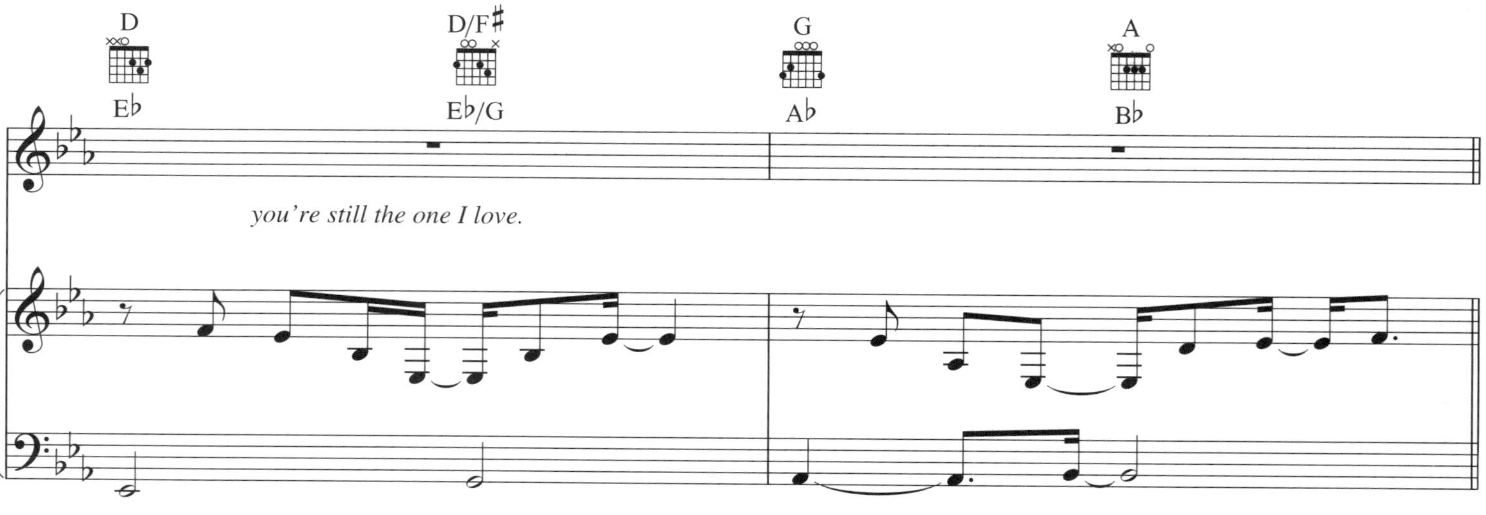

D
D/F♯
G
A
E♭
E♭/G
A♭
B♭
Looks like we made it. Look how far we've come, my ba - by.
Ain't noth - in' bet - ter, we beat the odds to - geth - er.
We might - a took the long way. We knew we'd get there some - day.
I'm glad we did - n't lis - ten. Look at what we would be miss - ing.
They said, "I bet they'll nev - er make it." But just
look at us hold - ing on. We're still to - geth -

D G A G
E♭ A♭ B♭ A♭
- er, still go - ing strong. (You're still the one.)
D G Em A
𝄋
E♭ A♭ Fm B♭
You're still the one I run to, the one that I be - long to.
D G A G
E♭ A♭ B♭ A♭
You're still the one I want for life. (You're still the one.)
D G Em A
E♭ A♭ Fm B♭
You're still the one that I love, the on - ly one I dream of.

D G A A
E♭ A♭ To Coda B♭ B♭
You're still the one I kiss good - night. night. You're still the one.
D G A D G
E♭ A♭ B♭ E♭ A♭
A G
B♭ A♭ D.S. al Coda
(You're still the one.)
CODA A
B♭
night.
D D/F♯ G A
E♭ E♭/G A♭ B♭
I'm so glad we made it. Look how far we've come, my ba - by.

THE GRAMMY AWARDS®
SONGBOOKS FROM HAL LEONARD

These elite collections of the nominees and winners of Grammy Awards since the honor's inception in 1958 provide a snapshot of the changing times in popular music.

PIANO/VOCAL/GUITAR

GRAMMY AWARDS RECORD OF THE YEAR 1958–2011

Beat It • Beautiful Day • Bridge over Troubled Water • Don't Know Why • Don't Worry, Be Happy • The Girl from Ipanema (Garôta De Ipanema) • Hotel California • I Will Always Love You • Just the Way You Are • Mack the Knife • Moon River • My Heart Will Go on (Love Theme from 'Titanic') • Rehab • Sailing • Unforgettable • Up, Up and Away • The Wind Beneath My Wings • and more.

00313603 P/V/G...$16.99

THE GRAMMY AWARDS SONG OF THE YEAR 1958–1969

Battle of New Orleans • Born Free • Fever • The Good Life • A Hard Day's Night • Harper Valley P.T.A. • Hello, Dolly! • Hey Jude • King of the Road • Little Green Apples • Mrs. Robinson • Ode to Billy Joe • People • Somewhere, My Love • Strangers in the Night • A Time for Us (Love Theme) • Volare • Witchcraft • Yesterday • and more.

00313598 P/V/G...$16.99

THE GRAMMY AWARDS SONG OF THE YEAR 1970–1979

Alone Again (Naturally) • American Pie • At Seventeen • Don't It Make My Brown Eyes Blue • Honesty • (I Never Promised You A) Rose Garden • I Write the Songs • Killing Me Softly with His Song • Let It Be • Me and Bobby McGee • Send in the Clowns • Song Sung Blue • Stayin' Alive • Three Times a Lady • The Way We Were • You're So Vain • You've Got a Friend • and more.

00313599 P/V/G...$16.99

THE GRAMMY AWARDS SONG OF THE YEAR 1980–1989

Against All Odds (Take a Look at Me Now) • Always on My Mind • Beat It • Bette Davis Eyes • Don't Worry, Be Happy • Ebony and Ivory • Endless Love • Every Breath You Take • Eye of the Tiger • Fame • Fast Car • Hello • I Just Called to Say I Love You • La Bamba • Nine to Five • The Rose • Somewhere Out There • Time After Time • We Are the World • and more.

00313600 P/V/G...$16.99

THE GRAMMY AWARDS SONG OF THE YEAR 1990–1999

Can You Feel the Love Tonight • (Everything I Do) I Do It for You • From a Distance • Give Me One Reason • I Swear • Kiss from a Rose • Losing My Religion • My Heart Will Go on (Love Theme from 'Titanic') • Nothing Compares 2 U • Smooth • Streets of Philadelphia • Tears in Heaven • Unforgettable • Walking in Memphis • A Whole New World • You Oughta Know • and more.

00313601 P/V/G...$16.99

THE GRAMMY AWARDS SONG OF THE YEAR 2000–2009

Beautiful • Beautiful Day • Breathe • Chasing Pavements • Complicated • Dance with My Father • Daughters • Don't Know Why • Fallin' • I Hope You Dance • I'm Yours • Live like You Were Dying • Poker Face • Rehab • Single Ladies (Put a Ring on It) • A Thousand Miles • Umbrella • Use Somebody • Viva La Vida • and more.

00313602 P/V/G...$16.99

THE GRAMMY AWARDS BEST COUNTRY SONG 1964–2011

Always on My Mind • Before He Cheats • Behind Closed Doors • Bless the Broken Road • Butterfly Kisses • Dang Me • Forever and Ever, Amen • The Gambler • I Still Believe in You • I Swear • King of the Road • Live like You Were Dying • Love Can Build a Bridge • Need You Now • On the Road Again • White Horse • You Decorated My Life • and more.

00313604 P/V/G...$16.99

THE GRAMMY AWARDS BEST R&B SONG 1958–2011

After the Love Has Gone • Ain't No Sunshine • Be Without You • Billie Jean • End of the Road • Good Golly Miss Molly • Hit the Road Jack • If You Don't Know Me by Now • Papa's Got a Brand New Bag • Respect • Shine • Single Ladies (Put a Ring on It) • (Sittin' On) the Dock of the Bay • Superstition • U Can't Touch This • We Belong Together • and more.

00313605 P/V/G...$16.99

THE GRAMMY AWARDS BEST POP & ROCK GOSPEL ALBUMS (2000–2011)

Call My Name • Come on Back to Me • Deeper Walk • Forever • Gone • I Need You • I Smile • I Will Follow • King • Leaving 99 • Lifesong • Looking Back at You • Much of You • My Love Remains • Say So • Somebody's Watching • Step by Step/Forever We Will Sing • Tunnel • Unforgetful You • You Hold My World • Your Love Is a Song • and more.

00313680 P/V/G...$16.99

ELECTRONIC KEYBOARD

THE GRAMMY AWARDS RECORD OF THE YEAR 1958-2011 – VOL. 160

All I Wanna Do • Bridge over Troubled Water • Don't Know Why • The Girl from Ipanema (Garôta De Ipanema) • Hotel California • I Will Always Love You • Just the Way You Are • Killing Me Softly with His Song • Love Will Keep Us Together • Rehab • Unforgettable • What's Love Got to Do with It • The Wind Beneath My Wings • and more.

00100315 E-Z Play Today #160 ....$16.99

PRO VOCAL
WOMEN'S EDITIONS

THE GRAMMY AWARDS BEST FEMALE POP VOCAL PERFORMANCE 1990–1999 — VOL. 57

Book/CD Pack

All I Wanna Do • Building a Mystery • Constant Craving • I Will Always Love You • I Will Remember You • My Heart Will Go on (Love Theme from 'Titanic') • No More "I Love You's" • Something to Talk About (Let's Give Them Something to Talk About) • Unbreak My Heart • Vision of Love.

00740446 Melody/Lyrics/Chords.................$14.99

THE GRAMMY AWARDS BEST FEMALE POP VOCAL PERFORMANCE 2000-2009 – VOL. 58

Book/CD Pack

Ain't No Other Man • Beautiful • Chasing Pavements • Don't Know Why • Halo • I Try • I'm like a Bird • Rehab • Since U Been Gone • Sunrise.

00740447 Melody/Lyrics/Chords.................$14.99

MEN'S EDITIONS

THE GRAMMY AWARDS BEST MALE POP VOCAL PERFORMANCE 1990-1999 – VOL. 59

Book/CD Pack

Brand New Day • Can You Feel the Love Tonight • Candle in the Wind 1997 • Change the World • If I Ever Lose My Faith in You • Kiss from a Rose • My Father's Eyes • Oh, Pretty Woman • Tears in Heaven • When a Man Loves a Woman.

00740448 Melody/Lyrics/Chords.................$14.99

THE GRAMMY AWARDS BEST MALE POP VOCAL PERFORMANCE 2000-2009 – VOL. 60

Book/CD Pack

Cry Me a River • Daughters • Don't Let Me Be Lonely Tonight • Make It Mine • Say • Waiting on the World to Change • What Goes Around...Comes Around Interlude • Your Body Is a Wonderland.

00740449 Melody/Lyrics/Chords.................$14.99

Prices, contents, and availabilbility subject to change without notice.

HAL•LEONARD® CORPORATION

7777 W. Bluemound Rd. P.O. Box 13819 Milwaukee, WI 53213

www.halleonard.com

1212